GENERAL THEORY OF ALIENS

Revealing the Truth of the Alien Phenomenon

Alex Xender Hum, Ph.D.

Cover designed by Alex Xender Hum

This book is a work of fiction. Names, characters, places, and incidents either are products of the author's imagination or are used fictitiously. Any resemblance to actual persons, living or dead, events, or locales is entirely coincidental.

Alex Xender Hum, Ph.D.
Visit my website at www.GeneralTheoryofAliens.com

Printed in the United States of America

First Printing: November 2018
Eye In The Sky Informatics

ISBN-9781730 881480

Contents

Illustrations

-1

Preface

*

Crystal-clear concepts generate in my thoughts all the time about the mysteries of Aliens and UFOs– why they are here; what can I learn from them, what are they telling me, and more. It's like an always-on data link with my consciousness, built up upon a sequence of deep thinking, follow-on research and reflections throughout my every moment.

An Electrical Engineer and Chief Enterprise Architect with many years of helping companies discover new commercial values and products, global digital and mobile solutions, and enterprise business platforms across a few industries, and an enthusiast of science, anthropology and ancient history, I am deeply fascinated by the distinct parallels between the worlds of Aliens and UFOs and Enterprise Architecture and Information Technology (IT).

My aim with this book is to bring out these parallels, explain them, and to change how we could now start to appreciate and understand the Alien and UFO phenomena and connect them to the context of Aliens as "Master Architects" of the Universe.

There have been a few theories about how our past has been shaped or even influenced by extra-terrestrial visitors who came to Earth with advanced knowledge, technologies and with various intentions over the eons. Whether they came with peace or with other higher purposes is something I have explored. I have enjoyed stories and theories from experts in various fields.

There is, however, one thing that bothers me a lot and it is that there is no theory yet that serves to unify and glue the entire "Alien and UFO" topic together into a consistent flowing story or hypothesis. This calling commits me into motion to write this book and to be the first person to propose the "General Theory of Aliens".

The content of the book may evolve over time possibly with new evidence and refinements to my theory. This is the start. I believe my book meets the high standards for out-of-the-world interests and curiosities seeking the truth in the minds and pursuits of extra-terrestrial phenomena.

This book contains my own thoughts and views. I write them down to amuse and inform myself first and foremost, to entertain my family and friends, and to challenge myself as I often try to find the one truth to bind all truths into a general unified theory, like Albert Einstein's General Theory of Relativity that binds cosmic relations between particles, life and the cosmos. I am respectful of people with other ideas and I am prepared to accept them as I expect them to be respectful and open to accept mine.

It would really be nice should my work start a new domain of scholarly pursuits, academic and commercial research across the world. Perhaps one day, I could be a contributor to the illuminating journeys of like National Geographic, History, Discovery, as we together spearhead, explore and further my theory, research and discover more.

There won't be this book without the constant encouragement of my loved ones and the pursuit of joy of doing it for them and for myself. Huge appreciation to them all. I dedicate this book to the fans and supporters throughout the whole spectrum of existence and consciousness, local and universal. And I thank everyone who supports me in any way, big or small or none, Aliens and/or humans and/or things. I want to get started ...

0

Introduction

*

"A'KIRA looks into the sky, then looks down at her hands and a crystalline Portal opens up from nothingness."

ENGAGE YOUR CURIOSITY. This book is a collection of my own theories of the possibilities, the what-ifs, the maybes, and the beliefs. Open your mind, open the doors and enter this domain to new ideas about how our past, thousands and millions of years ago, have contributed to our present and the future, and potentially also back to our past.

There have been theories about how our past has been shaped or even influenced by extra-terrestrial visitors who came with advanced knowledge and technologies. Either they came with peace or a higher purpose is what I will reveal.

There have been theories about Ancient Aliens - who they might be, where they came from, why and how they came, what their intentions are/were, why they travelled/are travelling light-years through space and time or dimensions, why they took enormous risks, their interactions with humans - many questions and certainly with many possible answers. In fact, more questions arose with seemingly multiple loops and layers of light-touch reasonings requiring stronger answers and in cases, generated many more questions with no answers. All good.

There is no meaningful unified way to explain these Ancient Alien theories. Questions have always been offered with localized geographical or cultural context related to where these Ancient Alien artefacts or anomalies were discovered. Never has there been offered a general theory that can unify all Ancient Alien theories, be it fact or fiction. I intend to bridge and fill that void with my book.

I feel there is a need for a general theory to unify all individual theories. Every endeavor follows a master plan, I call this the "Universal Solution Architecture". My General Theory of Aliens aims to provide the over-arching architecture as to how we can understand, study, explain and interpret the past, present and future discoveries of Ancient Alien artefacts.

Before I begin, I ask why these Ancient Aliens have come to Earth and left behind all these artefacts of technology or various depictions about their existence. I don't think Ancient Aliens are here without a meaningful reason nor even a plan. What is this plan? Why do Ancient Aliens travel potentially enormous amounts of light-years across the vast expanse of the known universe or universes, overcome unsurmountable risks and expended unimaginable amounts of resources to come to a tiny planet called Earth in this Solar System? Or is it only our Earth these aliens have visited? I think not to the latter.

As we look at Earth and at the stars above, what do we really see? What I say is we should also be 'seeing' the multitude of potential alien-visited planets. I stress on 'alien-visited' planets. Planets which are like Earth or at least similar in habitats to Earth. But not everyone sees the same thing or see things in the same way. That's ok.

The discoveries of technologies seemingly attributed to Ancient Aliens, the depictions of tall elongated figures and flying saucers found on cave paintings of thousands of years old, magnificent ancient monuments must be related and connected to each other, must have come from a single source or at least they are connected as part of a cosmic roadmap serving a higher purpose. What higher purpose might it be? Its plan and purpose must be greater than the sum of their individual discoveries and theories. Is there a unifying theory to make sense of everything?

My book will reveal what the plans of the Ancient Aliens are and their unifying purpose. I will provide explanations how the "Universal Solution Architecture" plan is designed, developed, implemented, executed and deployed not just on any one location but all over in and around the planet Earth and potentially other off-worldly planets too.

"STRANGE unknown symbols appear by magic, assembling into beautiful meaningful floating patterns."

1

Precious Mind, Precious Life

✳

"THE Portal imprints into A'kira's All-Seeing-Mind and manifests a series of warm and inexplicable symbols, waiting for inputs."

We are entitled, indeed we ought to think through hypotheses or theories, for if existing ideas or even theories are not called into question, research will be at an end. If new aspects or patterns of existing theories turn up, the old working or accepted hypotheses, however familiar or accepted it may have become, must be superseded or replaced by a new and better one. It seems the moment has come to introduce the first working hypothesis and place it at the very center of our research into aliens, what I call "General Theory of Aliens".

What sort of galactic data and knowledge would intelligent alien beings think about when they need to preserve and protect them so much? What could be so precious that these alien beings need to safeguard above all else that they are even willing to risk the unimaginable to dedicate their existence to design, deliver and deploy a multi-million-year strategy? Is it biological life? Is it wealth? Are Aliens protecting artificial life? Is it galactic memory or archives of all known historical events or future events yet to come? Does it have anything to do with life's wisdom or the protection of life or even the governance of existence itself or perhaps our *minds and souls*?

There is a kind of dimension to existence that guides thoughts and actions, and also a kind of dimension that governs the consequences of actions and inactions to further guide and I would say transform the next life onto the path of rightful existence. The dimension of Karma as Life's Teacher and Messenger.

The question is what kind of existence is worth protecting. What about particles? They are plenty of those. Countless stars and everything else in the Cosmos produce particles and are made of them. Particles come into existence and they leave it in multitudes of various forms. Do these particles know they existed even for a split iota of a human second? Does the Big Bang know its own existence?

I believe Alien beings are defending and protecting the true meaning of existence and are preserving existence's wisdom to pass it on to future worthy civilizations to learn from and to build on. Very much like chapters, sections and pages of an ever-flowing book of life. We do that ourselves, we have libraries, literary and scientific works, research and philosophy and Aliens do it on a much grander scale and with god-like purpose.

I am certain that these Alien beings had long realized that if existence is not protected and prepared for passing on to later generations of existential entities with consciousness, there will be no meaningful meaning for any prolonged existence at all. Things will just come and go and disappear, return back into nothingness. All that knowledge and wisdom will be lost forever. Forever going on a galactic repeat loop. All the emotions and lessons learnt that had guided every facet of existence, into the right, into the wrong, into the meaningless and pointless and all that are in between, will have been lost to the decay of memory, time and space forever. This is common facts of life unless something is done about it. The wisdom of not having to re-learn everything from day one but to start your platform from the Alien's past experiences, our past experiences, is what needs protecting and crucially to pass them on.

I believe these alien beings are preserving, defending and protecting the MINDS and SOULS of every entity, of everything who and that are born, lived, died, and reborn.

△ △ △

"I think, therefore I am"

René Descartes, also known as Renatus Cartesius (Latinized), was a very renown French philosopher, mathematician and scientist, who lived from 31 march 1596 to 11

February 1650. Descartes' works on philosophy and mathematics perhaps garnered the most exquisite insights into birth, life, death and rebirth.

In the beginning, Descartes arrived at only a single first principle: I think. Thought cannot be separated from me, therefore I exist. Most famously, this is known as *Cogito Ergo Sum* (English: "I think, therefore I am"). Therefore, Descartes came to the conclusion that, if he/she doubted, then something or someone must be doing the doubting, therefore the very fact that he/she doubted proved his/her existence. "The simple meaning of the phrase is that if one is skeptical of existence, that is in and of itself proof that he does exist." These two principles – I think and I exist – were later confirmed by Descartes's clear and distinct perception (delineated in his Third Meditation): that I clearly and distinctly perceive these two principles, Descartes reasoned, ensures them unquestionable. In other words, Descartes concludes that he can be certain that he exists because he thinks.

Descartes investigated the connection between mind and body, and how the two interact. One of his main influences for *dualism* was physics. The theory on the dualism of mind and body is Descartes's signature doctrine and permeates other theories he advanced. Known as *Cartesian Dualism* (or Mind-Body Dualism), it embraced the idea that mind (soul) and body are distinct but closely connected.

Descartes was a *rationalist* and believed in the power of *innate ideas*[1]. Descartes debated the theory of *innate knowledge* and that all human beings were born with knowledge and the ability to think by the virtue of a higher power.

What if this 'higher power' and 'innate knowledge' have something to do with Aliens? What if Descartes is an Alien being or perhaps he descended from Aliens to impart his theories to us? Now, what if Aliens had been keeping and protecting minds/souls or the 'innate knowledge' preparing it to impart and for transfer them to living beings? What if Aliens had somehow found a way to encode minds and souls into tangible entities, something that could bridge the physical with the metaphysical? And what if Aliens can store minds, souls or 'innate knowledge', where would they be stored? And how would they be stored and in what media?

---

[1] Innatism is a philosophical and epistemological doctrine that holds that, at birth, the mind is born with ideas/knowledge, and that therefore the mind is not a "blank slate".

Infinitely ever-expanding Data and Information

On our present-day Earth, we, humans and machines alike, generate lots of data and all kinds of data. We create all kinds of data every iota of our day and night, be it emails, music, pictures, movies, files, etc. We are content generators, content creators and we are also content receivers and transmitters. We never stop creating data. We never stop producing data and information belonging to our everyday lives. And we never stop storing our data or even backup data with multiple copies. Our smartphones and smart watches store everything about our movements, thoughts, actions and almost everything else, including the objects that have become part of our lives. We have entered the age of *IOT* (Internet of Things). Now, where do we store all these 'living' data, all these contents? We store all our data on our computers, smartphones, in the cloud. Enterprises store enormous amounts of data, often quoted in peta-bytes, in thousands of square-meters of multi-level data centers. Enterprises store data in the data centers we call the "Cloud".

These cloud-based data centers are built with thousands of computers, called servers, and are networked together in vast factory spaces in various locations across cities on Earth. Hundreds of kilometers of computer network cables connect all these servers into a meaningful data-sharing network to provide functions of computing, storage and bandwidth (see Figure 1). Thousands of data centers are built all over our planet. Some are built in cities, some deep in mountains, almost all are separated tens or hundreds of kilometers apart to prevent them being destroyed together so to preserve the storage of data in them should natural or man-made disasters happen to destroy these data centers storing all the 'precious' data and to ensure the continuity of computer needs required of them by enterprises, government or mission critical applications. This rule of architecture design of data centers is called 'Redundancy and Resilience'.

Figure 1: Data Centers - Built to store and process data. Countless racks of inter-connected computer servers providing functions of computing, storage and networking to the world.

I believe the *General Theory of Aliens (GTA)* is primarily about safeguarding and preserving the existence of life, minds and souls of every entity across the cosmos. I am proposing the **GTA** as my "Universal Alien Architecture Framework" and I will be using this framework to explain the general and special phenomenon of Aliens and UFOs, and to bring a never-before-attempted, yet a very much-needed and an overdue understanding to what the Aliens' "Universal Solution Architecture" is, the nature of which Aliens are so adamant to ensure the fabric of wisdom and knowledge of life and existence to never cease nor be destroyed, to continuously be transferred and never to be extinguished by the test of time and wills, to which end they have gone to extreme efforts over millions of years to achieve and to keep 'the lights on' through all time and space. Aliens understand the meaning of life to the highest order, and setting it on a course of meaning, purpose and fairness would need guidance and corrections like governance of "Cause and Effect". Holistically, I believe our Aliens have implemented a universal Karma engine.

In the next chapter, I will reveal the types of technology Aliens exploited to build their universal planetary and galactic data centers. These are not the normal data centers that we have today. These are what I call "Alien Data Centers" (ADCs). Aliens are still building them today as they ensure the continuation of the survival and propagation of knowledge and wisdom of the existence of everything.

"A'KIRA adjusts some standing parameters and a stream of thought patterns formed."

2

Alien Data Centers
◎ Crystals, Fire and Ice ◎

✳

"SOMETHING unexpected happened. Jyu-n's left hand is disappearing, it phases between solid and gas. Why are his fingers shriveling up?"

OMINIPRESENT HUMMING EVERYWHERE. No moving parts in sight. Something is moving but then nothing is moving. It is 'dark' everywhere except for some specks of light in the visible spectrum. There is a certain sense of activity at every level though not perceivable in the human sense. Something is moving, yet nothing moves.

△ △ △

Internet Data Centers

A Data Center (DC) is a facility used to house computer systems and related components such as telecommunications, networking and storage systems. Data centers generally include extra systems for redundancy and are designed with various backup components and infrastructures with continuous and uninterruptible power supply (UPS), data communications interfaces, environmental controls such as air conditioning and fire suppression and multitudes of security devices. For measures, a large data center is an industrial-scale operation requiring lots of resources - as much electricity as a small town, thousands of computers and thousands of kilometers of data cables and banks and banks of batteries, a few hectares of land space, and carefully chosen geographical locations.

The proliferation of commercial and personal interests in computers since the 1940s led to the beginning of a complex ecosystem consisting of computer systems and programmers. More so that a special environment was needed to operate and maintain it. New methods were needed to accommodate and organize the architecture of the computing infrastructure such as standard server racks[2] to mount standard-sized computing equipment, raised floors to aid with cooling and heat channeling, and cable trays installed overhead or under the elevated floor. A single server rack could house servers, network switches, storage medium or other computing devices. Powering up all the devices on a single rack requires a great deal of power and very importantly had to be accurately temperature-controlled and cooled to prevent overheating that could crash computing operations. As computers became increasingly expensive and the data it stores extremely priceless, security of data centers and of personnel working there, became the upmost of importance. As you can imagine, data centers very quickly became the life-line of many a mission-critical organization such as those for military or national defense purposes, business enterprises, public utility, civil security, transport, government, banking and financial institutions, medical facilities, airports, and more. Increasingly, governance around security, guidelines and principles for data center architecture design were devised and became a total necessity all over the planet.

---

[2] The standard server rack, based on the EIA (Electronic Industries Alliance), is a 19 inch (482.60mm) wide rack enclosure and 36 inches (914.40mm) deep with rack mount heights measured in rack units called "U" where 1U is 1.75" (44.45mm) high. A 42U rack, commonly used in data centers, would have an internal rack height of 73.5 inches (1.8669m). (See Figure 1)

From the early 1970s, the advent of *Unix* led to the proliferation of freely-available *Linux* PC (Personal Computer) operating systems in the 1990s. The latter were called "servers" giving rise to a new networking model called the "client-server" model, whose software architecture could facilitate the sharing of unique resources amongst thousands of users. The availability of inexpensive networking equipment, enabled by new and better standards for network structured cabling, made it all possible to use a hierarchical design that centralized servers in a specific room which inadvertently lead to the birth of the "data center".

What caused the boom of data centers? The dot-com bubble of 1997-2000 is the cause. Internet companies needed fast internet connectivity and non-stop operations with "always on" interactions with their consumers and suppliers to establish their foothold on the internet. The rate of data growth was so tremendous that installing your own computer rooms was no longer a commercial possibility for small companies nor absolutely a practicality for internet start-up companies. Many large and well-to-do companies started building very large facilities, called Internet Data Centers (IDCs), such as Amazon. IDCs provide commercial clients with a range of computing solutions and software for systems deployment such as servers and operations of their applications to every corner of the planet. Ever new technologies and best practices were applied to manage the scale and expansive operational requirements of such large-scale operations.

With the rise of ever-increasing consumer demand for more applications like social media, photo-sharing, blogs and forums, fan sites, video-sharing platforms, etc. a new kind of data center was needed, leading to the birth of the Cloud Data Centers (CDCs). There is an ever-expanding use of CDCs, and increasingly more of them, to produce new application areas of Artificial Intelligence (AI) and Machine Learning (MI) to industries like Oil and Gas, Finance, Banking, Retail, Logistics, Pharmaceutical, Aviation and Aerospace, Agriculture and everything else. To add to the huge demand for CDCs come the latest technologies like Blockchain, Autonomous Vehicles, and IOT (Internet of Things) and new revolutionary domains like Industry 4.0. There does not seem to be an end for more and more data centers with ever greater powers of computing, networking (enabled by fiber optical cables and high-speed ultra-bandwidth mobile wireless links), bandwidth and storage capabilities. It is easy to imagine that new types of data centers with ever more advanced technologies will be invented in the future to meet our exponential demands for data, zero-latency communication networks and ultra-high processing speeds. Or has it already been invented and in full operations, somehow hidden from us?

There is a special kind of data centers called the "Dark Data Center", also known as the 'lights out' data center or a 'darkened' data center. The Dark Data Center is a data center that has all but eliminated the need for direct access by engineers or computer personnel, except under extraordinary circumstances. As there is no need for staff to enter the data center for most of the time, it can be operated totally without lighting or much human-related facilities. All computing devices or devices to support the facility to operations running and maintenance are accessed and managed off-site by remote systems, relying on automation programs designed to perform unattended operations and surveillance. What are the advantages of a DCC? There are savings on energy consumption, reduction in staffing costs and the simplicity to locate the site further from population centers saving land and building costs for example in oceans, lakes or in space or even on asteroids. The other advantage is a Dark Data Center reduces the threat of malicious attacks and breaches, be it physical or digital, upon the infrastructure as the lesser the number of people who know its existence or location or nature, the better.

To cover the design principles and the multitude of system architectures of modern data centers, it will take many chapters, maybe I would have to write a new whole book, an endeavor which I think I will leave to another time perhaps. Well, for our present purpose, it is sufficed for me to say, some of the most *important considerations for data center design* are:

- o Site location;
- o Mechanical engineering infrastructure design;
- o Electrical engineering infrastructure design;
- o Telecommunication infrastructure design;
- o Availability;
- o Robustness;
- o Resilience;
- o Reliability;
- o N+1 redundancy;
- o No single point of failure;
- o Security;
- o Authorized personnel access, access control;
- o Security surveillance, Sensors;
- o Modularity and flexibility;
- o Environmental control (temperature and humidity control);
- o Miniature conducting whisker growths on metallic casings;
- o Electrical power systems including uninterruptible power supplies and backups like rows and rows of battery banks;
- o Fire protection with active and passive elements;
- o Greenhouse gas emissions;
- o Renewable energy and energy reuse;
- o Energy use and efficiency;
- o Power and cooling;
- o Thermal zone mapping; and the ultimate consideration,

o   The *Green* Data Center.

Very large data centers can occupy an entire building of at least 100,000 square foot or even over a few buildings or high-rise towers, and usually packed densely with 50,000 to 80,000 servers and maybe more. To have some perspective on the energy needs of data centers, in 2014 US data centers consumed about 70 billion kilowatt-hours of electricity. This represents 2% of the country's total energy consumption whose amount is equivalent to that consumed by about 6,400,000 average American homes that year. This is a 4% increase in total data center energy consumption from 2010 to 2014 (Sverdlik, Here's How Much Energy All US Data Centers Consume, 2016). There was a huge increase from the preceding five years during which the total US data center energy consumption grew by 24%. There was an even bigger change from the first half of the last decade when the US energy consumption grew nearly 90%.

While energy efficiency improvements have helped to tame the growth rate of energy consumption of US data centers and will have saved 620 billion kWh between 2010 and 2020, researchers expect the total US data center energy consumption to grow by 4% between 2016 and 2020, predicted to reach to about 73 billion kWh.

Servers are getting faster and better but at the same time, major cloud infrastructure providers like Google, Microsoft Azure, Amazon Web Services and Oracle (Sverdlik, Oracle Expanding New Cloud Platform to 13 Regions by 2019, 2018) are building more and even bigger data centers all over the work to meet burgeoning demands. How will they cope with meeting demands? To save the planet, should we cap our data growth, set a global quota per nation or stop everyone from using computing devices and smartphones? For many countries, data growth is synonymous with economic growth, the well-being of the population and businesses. Stopping or slowing down the growth and demands for data will be difficult. Possibly, I believe going down this route could one day lead to a Global Data Wars.

△ △ △

Data Center Transformation: Inevitability

Data Center Transformation is the process to modernize data centers to take advantage of the increasing performance and energy efficiency afforded by newer and more powerful computing equipment, software and capabilities such as "Cloud Computing".

Cloud computing is a class of computing on a massive scale which relies on shared pools of computer resources and services that is rapidly provisioned and deployed with minimal management effort often over the internet, resources like configurable computer servers, development tools, virtual machines, hot and cold storage medium and capabilities, load balancers, firewalls, VPNs (Virtual Private Networks), database, thin clients, mobile apps, web browser, operating systems, the list goes on.

Cloud computing allows enterprises to design, test and deploy their applications and get them running faster, ease of cost management, with improved manageability and less maintenance and allows IT (Information and Technology) teams to more rapidly adjust or scale up or down computing resources to meet ever-changing and unpredictable business demands. Cloud computing is growing at an unprecedented rate thanks to the availability of high-capacity telecommunication networks, low-cost computers at commodity prices and ever-faster storage devices as well as ubiquitous application of hardware virtualization, microservices, containerization, Application Programming Interface (APIs), Service-Oriented Architectures (SOA), open standards for data, human-centric programming languages, serverless architectures and ever-simple design-setup-and-go service models.

Cloud-computing providers, the people who setups and runs cloud computing facilities and cloud data centers, offers a "pay-per-use" or "pay-as-you-go" pricing or subscription models and based on the "sizing" – process power of server's CPUs (Central Processing Units), size and type of RAM, amount of storage (SDDs, HDDs) - to suit the needs of the customers' architecture of their enterprise applications.

Cloud-computing has seen fast advances with various providers offering multitude of computing models, service models and subscription pricing models. To simplify and unify approaches, cloud-computing providers now offer their services according to three main standard service models – Infrastructure as a Service (IaaS), Platform as a Service (PaaS) and Software as a Service (SaaS). To increase adoption of cloud-computing, these three models abstract their services as *layers* in a platform stack[3]. For example, a provider can provide SaaS implemented on bare-metal physical machines without using underlying PaaS or IaaS layers, and conversely one can run a program or cloud application on IaaS and access it directly without wrapping it as SaaS. Over time to meet expanding market needs and a result of entrepreneurship, other services models sprouted up making up "everything as a service" such as IOT as a Service (IOTaaS), Mobile backend as a Service (MBaaS).

---

[3] A digital platform stack or software stack is a set of software components or subsystems carefully architected to operate effectively together to create a complete platform that enables the execution of business applications to "run on top of" the resulting stack.

There are three main deployment models to operate a cloud computing platform. "Private Cloud" is a cloud-based infrastructure operated solely for a single organization, where it can be managed internally or externally by a third party, and hosted either internally or externally (with other clients in a large data center but operated in discrete silos for security purposes). The second deployment model is "Public Cloud" where the cloud services are rendered over a network that is open for public use. The third deployment model is a hybrid or composition of the first two deployment models, and aptly named as the "Hybrid Cloud". It could also be a case of maintaining important and highly-confidential databases locally or on-premise (within the organization's data center) and connecting them to the "Public Cloud" via high-speed high-bandwidth and secure telecommunication networks usually protected by VPN servers to secure the data links using data encryption and protection. With the huge demand in networking speeds, for lower and lower latencies, and agility to build out new, re-configure and replace network routings, cloud providers and telecommunications companies have expediently transformed to Software-Defined Networking (SDN). Conventional single-purpose network servers at data centers and in enterprise premises have transited to a universal device model orchestrated from a centralized cloud platform, and gradually being replaced by 'white boxes' commodity server equipment that can now deliver all routing functions as Virtual Machines (VMs) in one single box – functions like fire-wall, VPN, load balancers, security can now all be virtualized. In addition, extra Value Added Services (VAS) can be downloaded from a centralized App Store, re-configured on-the-fly and run on these boxes - VAS like Deep Packet Inspection (DPI), bandwidth aggregation, Edge Computing, and more. With rapid disruptive transformations in telecommunications, it is inevitable that data centers are evolving faster than before.

Industrial research puts the average age of a data center at nine years old, while Gartner, another research company, thinks data centers older than seven years are obsolete. The exponential increase of data - 163 zettabytes or 163, 000,000,000 Terabytes (TBs) by 2025 – is one of the largest contributing factors driving the modernization and transformation of data centers.

I believe Moore's law has a part to play with the inevitable evolution of our data centers, at least maybe till 2025. Moore's law is the keen observation that the number of transistors in a dense integrated circuit (IC) chip (computer processor chip, the brains of the computer) doubles every two years. Originally proposed by Gordon Moore, he initially described the doubling of every year but later, after a few decades, revised his forecast to doubling every two years. Although Moore's law is an observation and projection of a historical trend and not a physical or natural law, it was nonetheless a good guide to semiconductor advances, probably used also as a goal for the semiconductor industry and commercial competitiveness advantage. The projection cannot be sustained indefinitely as there is a limit to how close we can manufacture ICs with transistors with closer and closer gates in smaller and smaller nodes, and with a reasonably acceptable yield. Complementing micro-processor technologies with advanced software architecture, hyperscaling, and use of exotic materials for semiconductor designs could actually lead to more advances in computer performance.

What will data centers evolve into next to spearhead the next wave of industrial and consumer revolutions? How will that be done? What is the possible future direction? Let's take a look ...

$$\triangle \ \triangle \ \triangle$$

Alien Data Centers

How would you store information that constitutes Existence? Today's technology is quite capable to enable the storage of raw and repurposed digital media in the data centers. Any cloud-based storage applications and appliances are hosted in earth-based data centers. All the data, pictures, images, files, photographs are stored in physical media which are in turn realized by actual physical storage devices like magnetic tapes, magnetic Hard Disk Drives (HDDs), Solid State Devices (SSDs), that are able to store trillions and trillions of bits and bytes of 0s and 1s. When you need more storage, you add more storage devices.

What kind of materials would intelligent Alien beings use to construct massive storage facilities that their Alien Data Centers are built on? These beings would need materials that are freely available and easily assembled with as little need to manage as possible across large distances and time latencies and which comes with super ease of maintenance, possibly remotely. Some kind of construction that will just happen with minimal intervention and supervision as practically possible. Something that would just grow out of nothing, organize itself and something that only takes time and what's naturally available in the environment, like natural resources.

I believe Aliens build their data center facilities deep in the planet. I believe Aliens are using a very special kind of material. Storing 0s and 1s using today's electrical technologies is only good for data but not possible to store extra-dimensional data attributes like existential memories of the mind and wisdom that have multiple dependencies and inter-linkages that humans have not comprehended nor discovered yet. Memories are entities beyond videos, podcasts and images.

I believe Ancient Aliens grow their data centers out of crystals. They do not build them like how we build data centers. Yes, I believe these Alien Data Centers are not built but actually grown, like how trees, fruit trees, plants and vegetation are grown on dedicated facilities. Aliens built them by using some kind of self-replicating super-crystalline materials with a programmable computer core. What might these materials be, that fit into the above profile? I believe they are a special form of Crystals of some kind! These "Alien Crystals" are not manufactured like in today's factories but they actually grew and multiply in some kind of pre-determined configurations and in a replicating order with programmable properties that complies with some kind of their alienic primary code, possible like with a DNA.

△ △ △

Super Giant Crystal Caves

Crystals have many wondrous and still undiscovered properties that scientists are only scratching the surface of. Crystals respond and react to electrical signals and potentially to other forms of excitations as we shall discover. Crystals can generate electrical signals too and something exotic too. Actually, crystals are also able to store multi-dimensional information.

What are the likely places where we can find these crystals that we expect them to grow on command?

Over the last hundreds of years, humans have found crystal caves in many locations on this planet. The most famous one is called the "Cave of Crystals" located in Chihuahua, Mexico at a place called the Naica Mines (Figure 2). The "Cave of Crystals" lies about 290 meters (~967 feet) below the earth's surface deep in a volcano, and the cave contains never-before-seen giant crystal beams. Each column of crystal beam is about 11 meters (36 feet 8 inches) tall the size of pillars, about 1.2 meters (4 feet) across and weighing at least 55 tons (55,000 kilos). The color of the giant crystal beams is so beautiful, a kind of translucent galactic white.

Figure 2: "Cave of Crystals" - Giant crystals found in Naica Mines, Naica, Chihuahua, Mexico. Crystal beams with extreme heights, like skyscrapers.

These giant crystals are produced and carefully crafted by the magma below the caves, with the heat feeding huge caverns of water and crystalline-growing materials like gypsum (see Figure 3). These crystals are relatively young at about 500,000 years compared to universe's age of about 13.3 billion years old. The conditions in the caves are extreme, with inhumanly high temperatures of about 54°C. In fact, the sight of crystals in the caves and their abundant presences can be thought of like representing data centers of today, with their rows of server racks and equipment in hot rooms. Human explorers have to wrap themselves up in super cold highly-specialized protective suits packed with dry ice and breathing apparatus before they are allowed into the caves but can only stay for about 20 minutes. Explorers exiting the cave have to hibernate in cold rooms for hours to recover their strength and must hydrate with lots of fluids to bring back heath to their bodies.

The crystals were discovered by two miners in 2000. They were sent to excavate further into the mine to search for more minerals like silver, zinc and lead deposits. One thing to note is that back in 1910, some workers had actually discovered another spectacular crystal cave in the same Naica mines, but this time at a much shallower depth of about 120 meters (400 feet), almost half the depth of the one discovered in 2000 the "Cave of Crystals". This particular cave is called "Cave of Swords" and it is filled with many more different kinds of sharp and slender crystals but much smaller about 1 meter (3 feet 4 inch) long, in a cave 47°C hot.

Figure 3: Locations of the "Cave of Crystals" and "Cave of Swords" - Formations of giant Gypsum Crystals withing the Niaca Mines, Mexico.

According to discoverers, the Cave of Crystals is a *natural* void, one of many, deep in the heart of this particular Naica volcano. Natural? Maybe. I don't think they are natural at all. I think they were grown by Ancient Aliens who were exceptionally skilled in the technology and science of crystal manufacturing. The conditions for producing these giant crystals beams are purposely engineered by mixing the required conditions like high temperatures, pressure, earth minerals and water. Yes, water is an essential ingredient for making crystals! Actually, and lots of heat for the quality and quantity.

Crystal beams get larger, taller and heavier if they are formed deeper into the earth, and the longer you maintain the environment for their growth. Imagine the size of those at a depth of 1,000 meters or 2,000 meters! We can see a small sample of the type of Selenite Crystal Beams that can be found in the "Cave of Crystals" in Figure 4.

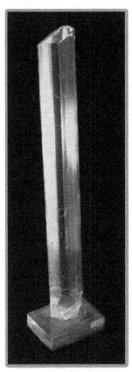

Figure 4: Selenite "Sword" - A small sample of the type of selenite crystal beam that can be found in the "Cave of Crystals" in Naica Mine, Mexico. This sample measures 22.6cm by 2.6cm by 1.6cm (8.90 inch by 1.02 inch by 0.63 inch).

Water is an important ingredient for the engineering and growth of crystal beams. This fact is hugely important because it means that planets without a natural source of water is impossible for the creation of crystals. Thinking further, this also means that crystals can only be created and found on planets that can sustain life! As scientists believe life needs water. This is an amazing revelation to enthusiasts searching for life-sustaining planets. No Crystals No Life! No Life No Crystals!

It can even be imagined that these conditions were already available for assembling Alien crystal data centers since the time the planet was formed billions of years ago. It just needs the alien technology to bring together the crystal-forming conditions into a right balance and configuration to deliver the right applications and functionality. Perhaps prehistoric tsunamis brought mineralized liquids into crevices in the bowels of volcanoes and had earthquakes sealed them up? I believe these conditions are brought forth by automated programs the Ancient Aliens had installed in their data centers and had kept it running in the eternal clock of existence. These automated programs could be a part of a pan-planetary terra-forming project, similar to what human is planning to colonize Mars and possibly other planets in the 'Goldilock' zone.

Depending on conditions, crystal beams can take tens or hundreds of thousands of years to form or could take days, weeks of months. It can be imagined that crystals production with far enough advancements could take much lesser time, perhaps in sub-seconds. Crystals are produced in many forms, with multi-sided beams or 'multi-termination point' tips, that are based on the strengths of their atomic bonds and environmental conditions. I believe Ancient Aliens are capable to manipulate crystals at the particle level to produce them to deliver whatever functions they are required for, be it for computing, networking, communications, storage or object manipulation or other advanced yet-to-be-discovered super properties. The amazing thing is the crystals can grow even bigger because there are no limits to the size and dimensions the crystals can grow to! (Lovgren, 2007) (Gramling, 2008)

Replacing or needing increasing storage or computing powers, the provisions of magma and water connected to a crystal cave or a new crystal cave will trigger the growth of more crystal beams on demand, perhaps similar to a kind of cloud subscription model that scales up computing functions on demand, perhaps like some kind of "Crystals-as-a-Service" for the sake of relating to modern-day cloud computing commercial technological business models and paradigms.

The *General Theory of Aliens (GTA)* is Aliens have mastered the capabilities and knowledge of how to build out their large caves of giant Crystals anywhere in the planet, have harnessed the super properties of crystals and knew how to grow giant crystal caves (Alien Data Centers) in any pre-determined and pre-configured manner and imbued them with super technological capabilities, with highly-advanced patterns of genetically architected to operate their data centers with computing prowess beyond our wildest dreams.

In the next chapter, I will share my theory on the inspirations of the ancient builders of ancient pyramids and obelisks during ancient times. A modern famous monument can help to light up the way.

"JYU-N expended an unnerving cry of exasperation, bordering on physical and spiritual pain. He immediately knew why but thought he had time."

3

Fascinated by Giant Crystals
⊡ The Great Obelisks ⊡

✳

"A'KIRA waves her mind moving the orb around a crystal cave, zooming in on a collective of orange blinking budding crystals. Diagnostics completed, performance tip-top."

Civilizations have always been amazed by the mysterious appearances and forms of crystals throughout all time. Crystals come in all forms and sizes. Some cultures, both ancient and modern, are so fascinated by crystals that they build models, some towering hundreds of meters into the sky, and some are even more massive. Have you ever wondered where majestic looking Obelisks of ancient Egypt get their shape from? Yes, obelisks get their shapes from the giant crystal beams, like those from the "Cave of Crystals" (Figure 2).

One of the most famous obelisks in the world stands at Washington, D.C., it is called the Washington Monument, built at the beginning of 1884. See Figure 5. It is also the world's tallest physical representation of a giant crystal beam, standing at about 169.30 meters (~564 feet). The Washington Monument is styled after Egyptian obelisks which are found populated throughout ancient Egypt. Now, question, where did the ancient Egyptians get their inspirations for the designs of their obelisks? I think they were inspired by what they 'saw' of alien-made giant crystal beams i.e. like those found in the "Cave of Crystals". I will reveal in Section "Alien Teachers and Messengers" on page 82 how Aliens and UFOs inspired ancient civilizations.

Figure 5: A True Obelisk - The Washington Monument at Washington D.C. This Obelisk stands as the world's tallest obelisk at a majestic height of 169.30 meters (~564 feet) tall. A truly magnificent 'single-termination point' Obelisk. (Alex X. Hum)

The world's more famous and ostensibly the largest obelisk is actually in Giza, Egypt. Let me explain. If the Great Pyramid of Giza brings awe to you, it should be. The uppermost piece or capstone of an obelisk is called a pyramidion. I believe the Great Pyramid of Giza is actually meant to be the pyramidion or tip of a super-giant "Great Obelisk". This "Great Obelisk" would actually be buried in the ground under the Great Pyramid. The size of this "Great Obelisk" would greatly dwarf that of the Washington Monument.

The first and largest of the Giza Pyramids was built by the pharaoh Khufu whose reign started around 2251 BCE. His pyramid, initially stood at 146.5m (488 feet 4 inch) tall, is called the "Great Pyramid of Giza" and is considered as one of the wonders of the world.

How tall do you think the "Great Obelisk" would be standing had it been built? The height of pyramidion of the Washington Monument is 16.6m (55 feet 4 inch) tall and the Great Pyramid is 146.5m (488 feet 4 inch) tall. By using the Law of Equivalence, this "Great Obelisk" in Giza, Egypt, would be standing at a majestically heavenly height of 1,503 meters (5010 feet) tall, making it the tallest man-made structure ever built. Just like the Washington Monument was built in phases, it can be imagined that the "Great Obelisk" in Giza, most likely will also be built in phases, would take a very long time to complete, it could probably take over 200 years. Too long to wait perhaps for the lifetime of a pharaoh waiting for this monument to commemorate his existence while he is living of course! Thus, only the pyramidion, which in this case is *the* Great Pyramid, was built but not the entire mega-structure of the "Great Obelisk".

Where is this "Great Obelisk"? Where can I see this gigantic crystal structure?

What would be an alternative way to be still having the "Great Obelisk" built with full knowledge that it will take two centuries to build it but want it within your lifetime? I think one clever way to do it is to 'build' this "Great Obelisk" is to actually site it below the ground! The shaft of the beam structure is actually under the surface with the Great Pyramid as its pyramidion tip sitting proudly above it and above ground! See Figure 6 for an illustration.

Another way to think about it is that obelisks are truly meant to be shaped like giant crystal beams to honor the powerful existence of crystal beams found in hidden Alien Data Centers. And that pyramids around the world, and possibly on other-worldly planets, are shaped like tips of giant crystal beams, that actually are the pyramidion tips of giant crystals!

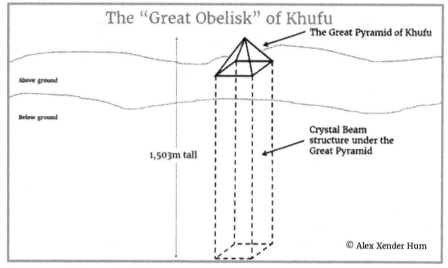

Figure 6:   The 'Great Obelisk' hidden underneath the Great Pyramid of Khufu at Giza, Egypt. (Alex X. Hum)

On the plains of Giza there are three giant pyramids. The largest pyramid is the Great Pyramid of Khufu, the second largest is the Pyramid of Khafre and the smallest of the three is the Pyramid of Menkaure. Following the previous line of thought, we can imagine there to be not one, not two but three "Great Obelisks", one under each of the three pyramids. This is mind-boggling! Can you imagine three super giant crystal obelisks under the ground in Giza, with one giant crystal obelisk under each of the three giant pyramids? Figure 7 illustrates the possible existences of the "Three Great Obelisks" of Giza.

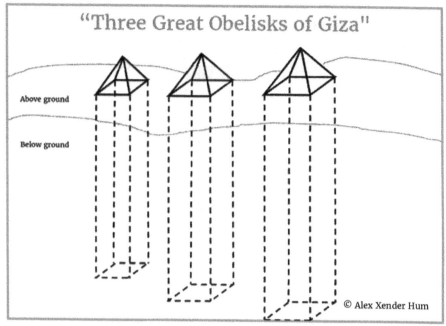

Figure 7: *"Three Great Obelisks" of Giza - One giant crystal obelisk, heights of hundreds of meters, under each of the three Great Pyramids of Giza. (Alex X. Hum)*

What will be their function for their existence? What do they serve? What do these giant structures have in common? Actually, they resonate at some certain frequencies where some scientists would say they give out a humming sensation. Why would they be arranged in threes? Are they part of a larger architecture, part of the "Universal Solution Architecture"? Are they part of a large architecture networks of communication infrastructure? Are these 'mind resonators' working together as a Yagi-Uda Antenna[4], bouncing waves off each element of the giant crystal beams, thus shaping the maximum efficiencies of transmissions and receptions?

Perhaps it is true that the goal of various ancient civilizations on Earth, particularly to the beliefs of the ancient pharaohs and Egyptians, was to construct and build the largest and tallest standing Obelisk that could ever be built, so much so as to rival all pharaohs' monuments. Well, actually it is not very different with what our modern society would still do today i.e. build the next tallest skyscraper or the longest suspension bridge, etc. It is not too far a stretch to believe that the ancient pharaoh's

---

[4] A Yagi-Uda Antenna is a directional antenna made of multiple parallel elements in a line. The radio waves from the multiple elements superpose and interfere to enhance radiation in a single direction, with a substantial increase in gain compared to a single dipole antenna.

goal was to focus on building the tallest pyramid instead of the tallest Obelisk because it would be too difficult to build the tallest standing Obelisk, not just because of its size and complexity, but because it would take centuries to do so. Therefore, the tallest pyramid, just the tip of the obelisk, would suffice to be the true representative of the intended super giant Obelisk that the pharaoh and the dynasty would have built. Another way of looking at it would be to take the belief that the ground-standing pyramid (as depicted in Figure 6) is the tip of the "Great Obelisk" as it was intended to be and in this case it was 'standing' beneath the ground surface something like some kind of an inverted Obelisk or a kind of 'double-termination point' crystal if we could call it that way. Truly exceptional discovery of an idea indeed.

The **General Theory of Aliens** is to know that, all over the ages and eons of civilizations, intelligent beings are fascinated by the Crystal form and they had spent their lifetime creating and building something truly amazing and wonderful, like mega-size monuments of pyramids and obelisks.

What is the significance in the forms and functions of these pyramids and giant obelisks?

Many ancient civilizations had been intrigued with the 'supernatural' powers of crystals (to be covered in Chapter "Incredible Powers of Crystals" on page 43) and had tirelessly dedicated their fascinations to constructing various forms and sizes of pyramid-like shapes millenniums ago. We will also take a look at Mesoamerican pyramid-shaped structures and other forms in Section "Alien Teachers and Messengers" on page 82.

In the next chapter, I will reveal the world's imaginative fascinations with devices made of crystals. Their forms and functions are out of this world!

"IN a flash, majestic soaring orange crystal beams shot up! A'kira deftly maneuvers Disk'ta darting loading up her new crystal chums."

4

High-Tech Devices of Super Crystals

"SPACE swallowed Disk'ta, phasing away with brilliant spectral lights. Disappearing into the Emptiness."

There are many parallel phenomena that portrays our artistic fascinations with crystals, across many cultures. Perhaps one of the most famous one can be attributed to a very famous and popular character, yes, he is Superman.

△ △ △

"Fortress of Solitude"

The "Fortress of Solitude" is a fictional fortress that appears in the Superman comic books series published by DC Comics. The "Fortress of Solitude", away from civilization, is a place of self-reflection, and an advanced technological and research laboratory for Superman. He often uses it to communicate and learn from the knowledge and wisdom stored in a copy of Kryptonian database kept there. The knowledge manifests itself in the form of an Artificial Intelligence (AI) entity.

Originally, the "Fortress of Solitude" was built into a mountain or in an underground complex in a mountainous cliffside. There are many editions of the Fortress written over the length of the comics stories. Some chapters put it at the bottom of ocean and in the Amazon Forest. Most traditionally in comic stories and movies nowadays, the "Fortress of Solitude" is now located somewhere in the Arctic.

Superman's "Fortress of Solitude" actually *grew* into existence or self-replicated at almost instantaneous speeds from a pre-programed crystal code out of a piece of handheld green crystal manufactured from his home planet of Krypton (See Figure 8). My view is that this "Superman Crystal" grew into a huge fortress-like crystalline structure imbued with advanced alien architecture with networks of security, high-tech chambers, sensors and extremely powerful AI computing abilities, basically like the kinds of Alien Data Centers that I am writing about in this book. As you know, all data centers, be it normal or alien ones, would need extreme layers of security and defenses to protect the precious data, knowledge and information stored in them.

Interestingly, the "Fortress of Solitude" is also referred as the "Fortress of Knowledge", referring it to the secure storage place of universal knowledge and teachings that Jor-El, the biological father of Superman, transmitted to Superman himself at birth and through his life on Earth.

Figure 8: Superman's "Fortress of Solitude" - Created by a Crystal from Krypton. I believe it is also a kind of Alien Data Center.

△ △ △

Crystal Skull

One other very interesting area of fascination with the super properties of crystals is the phenomenon of the "Crystal Skull". "Crystal Skull" is a hand-held object shaped like a skull of a human or in some cases shaped like a "Grey Alien". Most "Crystal Skulls" are life-size while some others are a few inches in diameter. See Figure 9 for an illustration.

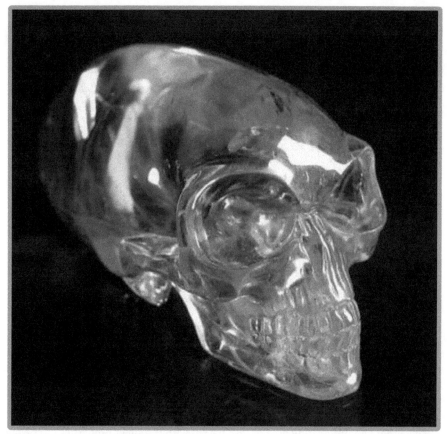

Figure 9:   Alien-form "Crystal Skull" - shaped like a "Grey Alien" and made of clear transparent white quartz from a solid monolithic block of crystal, presumably thousands of years old. Notice the elongated structure of the skull, supposedly to signify the storage of vast amounts of alien knowledge, wisdom and presumably of alien technological know-how collected throughout the Universe.

There are beliefs that Crystals Skulls have healing qualities, they emit some kind of psychic energy or auras or sounds, they have the ability to convey and share vital information and wisdom about the past, present and future like how crystal balls are used to seek out visions of events before they happen, and they could be repositories of ancient wisdom. Some believers refer to the Mayan creation myths of a story of 13 "Crystal Skulls" being scattered by Mayans thousands of years ago waiting to be discovered and reunited in times of need. I will illuminate on this point in Section "Human Crystals" on page 122 later on.

These "Crystal Skulls" are made of large and the most transparent clear quartz crystals. Since the middle of the nineteenth century, "Crystal Skulls" have generated great interests and fascination since they began to surface in public events, private collections and museums. The nature and history of their discoveries and accounts have been sketchy at best and often debated upon, with most accounts attributed to the Maya, Aztec or Mixtec eras. Various versions of the "Crystal Skulls" are exhibited or stored in museums around the work, such as the British Museum in London, the National Museum of American History at the Smithsonian Institution in Washington DC, the Museum de l'Homme in Paris. Since their discoveries, human-form "Crystal Skulls" have captured the imagination of enthusiasts the world over.

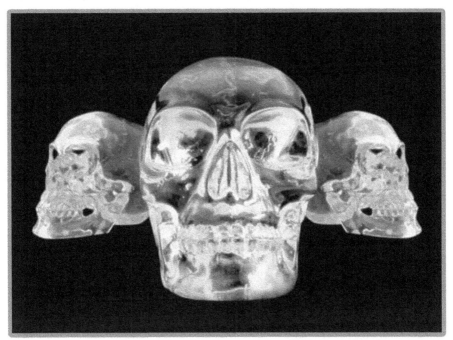

Figure 10: Human-form "Crystal Skulls" - Exhibited in museums around the world.

One may ask about the 'age' of a "Crystal Skull". As "Crystal Skulls" are supposedly 'carved' from a solid homogeneous block of a crystal monolith, its age would take the age of the crystal block it is made form. The ages of "Crystal Skulls" could range from a few thousand years old to at least over a million years old. Now, I believe it is logical and reasonable to think that the "Crystal Skull" would also take the super properties of the crystal monolith.

This is no evidence nor information of the source crystal material these "Crystal Skulls" are made from. *I would like to tease the idea of making a "Crystal Skull" out of one of the giant crystal beams we can find in the "Cave of Crystals", which I wrote about at the beginning of this chapter. It would be awesome and unbelievable if this could take realism.*

Some Crystal Skull enthusiasts point to the piezoelectric properties of quartz crystals as evident to the powers of the Crystal Skulls. They believe that the skulls might function like intricate computer chips that could have recorded the history of the Earth, or could even store and perhaps transmit the messages from Aliens or their lost civilizations to those who can 'read' it and possible to 'talk' to it. I think we just need to find the right method to interface with these "Crystal Computer Chips" and to communicate with them, to understand them and to learn from them.

The **General Theory of Aliens** is that Aliens have mastered the science of harnessing the properties of super crystals. They have the know-how to extend its inherent properties to any object made out of them. Break a computer chip in a modern PC or smartphone today will destroy the function of that object. But make an object or device out of a crystal beam will reproduce any broken master functions and perhaps have the ability to 'program' new features or modify existing ones and even to self-repair and self-heal like some crystals do.

In the next Chapter, I will reveal to you some of the most amazing and unbelievable but true super properties of crystals. Crystals do hold some very powerful properties that man are only staring to scratch the surface of.

"QUANTUM entanglements permeate between dimensions aiming for Axiom:Heart, a special tiny inhabited blue planet."

5

Incredible Powers of Crystals
◎ Conquering Quantum, Energy, Space and Time ◎

✳

"PULSATING CRYSTALS in Disk'ta producing a tranquil humming concerto, empowering her with brilliant energy turning invisible."

OUR COSMOS IS *REALLY* BIG, *REALLY, REALLY* BIG. Outer space has no real physical end in sight. Literally, there is no beginning and there is no end.

Alpha Centauri is the nearest star system to our own Solar System and it is more than 4 light years away. Light from the sun reaches earth in about 5 earth minutes. Travelling within our own solar system takes time and, with all the leftover planet-making materials floating the space between Earth and our intended destination, is difficult to plan.

With our current 'space-faring' technology, it would take us about 100 hundred earth years to reach Alpha Centauri. We don't have a spaceship that can go faster than the speed of light yet. With nuclear power, a limitless source of energy, we can only reach about 4.5% of the speed of light.

We need some kind of technology that can help us go faster-than-light (FTL) to crunch out the vast distances between stars. There may be some ideas that are based on real science and principles to design these creative methods of travel.

One potential method of FTL travel is based on utilizing Einstein-Rosen Bridges, which are also known as wormholes. Albert Einstein's general theory of relativity predicted wormholes, although we may have 'seen' them from a very far distance via highly-sensitive radiation-sensing equipment.

An Einstein-Rosen Bridge is a shortcut through space caused by the warping of space and time caused by the presence of massively-densed objects like stars or black holes which can bend space and time like how a bowling ball warps the surface of a trampoline but imagine it three-dimensionally. A massive enough object could bend the space-time continuum to create a direct connection between two points in space. Physicists like Stephen Hawking and Kip Thorne have theorized that wormholes could theoretically be stabilized with the right amount of energy to allow objects through. Crystals are used to create high-power lasers that emit huge quantities of light energy. What if super crystals could be used as a kind of power source for space travel to create wormholes?

Two other potential ways of FTL travel is by travelling through the Hyperspace (Star Wars) and by using Warp Drives (Star Trek). Both Hyperspace and Warp Drives travels describe a means of traveling way over the speed of light but both still take a quantifiable amount of time. This is apparent when the space-travelers in such spaceships had time to chill out and entertain themselves with board games.

Like an Einstein-Rosen bridge, warp technology cleverly skirts around the impossibility of accelerating a spaceship past the speed of light by bending space itself around the spaceship and then crossing it. Warp technology compresses the volume of space in front of the spacecraft and expends it behind. The Star Trek Enterprise basically rides a bubble of regular three-dimensional (3-D) space while the universe changes around it. In Star Trek techno-speak, warp factor One is equal to 1 × light speed akin to breaking the sound barrier but at the speed of light, warp Two is equal to 8 × the speed of light while warp Three is 27 × the speed of light. It works out that the warp factor N would be equal to N to the power of three i.e. N^3 times the speed of light. So, warp factor Four would work out to be $4 × 4 × 4 = 64$ times the speed of light. Warp Six is the common cruising speed for the USS Enterprise NCC-1701, so at $6 × 6 × 6 = 216$ times the speed of light. At tremendous speeds of faster-than-light travel, just like in the case of Einstein-Rosen bridge, warp travel would need huge amounts of energy or need to be powered by some kind of unknown exotic energy source in order to sustain this mode of FTL space travel. Star Trek 'solve' this energy source with a fictional element called *Dilithium* crystals, which is supposedly able to produce enormous, super volatile reactions of matter and anti-matter.

How about *not* travelling through the universe which, by the limits of laws of physics, does not allow faster-than-light travel? How about we travel through the *Hyperspace*. Hyperspace is best understood as a sub-region of our real space where the same physical laws do not apply. In the Star Wars movies, all kinds of vehicles are equipped with hyperspace drives, from small personal fighters like X-Wings, to larger freighters like the Millennium Falcon to the massive moon-sized space station called the Death Star. We often hear that Star Wars is space fantasy not science fiction. Thus, what powers their hyperspace engines is better not to speculate but good to know that hyperspace travelers have time to hang out and chat.

But what if you could get to another faraway part of space in no time at all? The Jump Drives in *Battlestar Galactica* made interstellar teleportation possible with virtually no delay. These FTL spaceships are powered by refined *Tylium*, a very rare ore that is 10 million times more energetic than gasoline.

Instantaneous teleportation is a convenient mode of travel in sci-fi stories. Star Trek uses it to 'beam' individuals between spaceships, and landing people and objects on planets or to any point in space. This mode of space travel does possibly have some roots in scientific theory. Shall we explore further?

△ △ △

Quantum Entanglement for Teleportation

Quantum entanglement is a phenomenon where groups of particles behave similarly even when separated by great distances of space. Einstein affectionately called this "spooky action at a distance."

In theory, we could 'teleport' a spaceship or a person or an object or any entity or a piece of information or data using the same kind of technology. It could get a bit more complicated. We would have to "transcribe" information at the quantum level from particles at source location in space and 'transfer' them to particles at the defined location at the destination.

For now, quantum entanglement is something we can observe on an extremely small scale. We are probably a long way from teleporting people or things. What if Aliens have actually found a way to achieve that?

Imagine Ancient Aliens had already mastered the technology to harness the power of crystals for their quantum computing abilities and are performing instantaneous teleportation very much akin to performing a Jump Drive. Or perhaps even more advanced capabilities than we could possibly imagine.

Quantum entanglement has been demonstrated experimentally with photons, neutrinos, electrons, molecules as large as buckminsterfullerene (C_{60}), and even small diamonds. The utilization of quantum entanglement in communication and computation is a very active area of research at the best of research laboratories around the world.

In July of 2017, it was reported that Chinese scientists (Emspark, 2017) have shattered a world record in teleportation. They sent a packet of information from Tibet to a satellite orbiting around Earth, up to 1,400 km (870 miles) about the Earth's surface. To be technically precise, the scientists *beamed* the quantum state of a photon – information about how it is polarized – into orbit.

The team set a record for the largest quantum teleportation distance and they also showed that one can build a practical system for long-distance quantum communications. With such a communication system, online communications or exchange of information would be impossible to be snooped or eavesdropped on without the users being alerted to the security breach. *Quantum communications would be ideal if data transfers and communications must be pure and highly accurate without any loss, tampering or hacking, like, for example, in the process of mind transfer which I had discussed in the previous chapter.*

Experiments like this one have been done before but this particular test extends and expands the possibilities and boundaries for quantum technology. The experiment makes use of one of several phenomena that describes quantum mechanics - it is quantum entanglement or "spooky action at a distance" as called by Albert Einstein. What is quantum entanglement? You see, when two particles are entangled, like 'connected' to each other not in a physical kind of way, probably metaphysically, they remained 'connected' so that an action performed on one of the two particles affects the other particle in a known way, no matter how far apart the two are. Along the same understanding, when a state of one of the two particles, say its spin or polarization, in the entangled duo is known by some kind of measurement, we would automatically know the state of the second 'connected' particle. What this means is that if we excite or modify the property of one of the two particles of the entangled duo, the other particle will be affected or changed in exactly the known way.

Physicists call the states "correlated," because if one particle – a photon, for example – is in an "up" state, its entangled partner will definitely be in a "down" state – a kind of mirror image. To be technically precise, there are four possible combinations for the two particles to be in: up-up, down-down, up-down and down-up. The interesting part of this entanglement phenomenon is that once the state of the first particle is measured, the second particle somehow 'knows' what state it should be in. The entangled information seems to travel instantaneously without limited by the speed of light and without any latency (delay of information travel).

△ △ △

Teleporting Quantum Information

In June of 2017, the same set of scientists reported another achievement in quantum teleportation – they sent entangled photons from the Micius Satellite to two ground stations over distances of between 1,600 and 2.400 km (994 and 1,490 miles), depending on the location of the satellite in orbit. Entanglement over long distances has been experimentally proven, the real deal is that now we can use entanglement to transmit a photon's quantum state to a receiver at any distant locations.

In their latest experiment, the same team of Chinese scientists fired a laser from the Ngari ground station in Tibet to a satellite in orbit. That laser beam carried a photon that is entangled with another photon on the ground station. They then entangled the photon on the ground station with a third photon and measured their quantum states. Now, the scientists on the ground station didn't reveal the states of the two photons on the ground station to anyone. They just asked whether their states were the same or different – in this case it would be either vertical or horizontal polarizations. Actually, there are four possible combinations of states: vertical-vertical, vertical-horizontal, horizontal-vertical, horizontal-horizontal. Since the states of the two particles on the ground were correlated with the one on the satellite, an astronaut observing the photon in the satellite would know that this photon would have to be in one of the four possible states that is correlated with the two photons on the ground station.

If there was an astronaut riding in the satellite, when this person was told that the states of the ground-based photons were the same or different, the astronaut would know enough to reconstruct the state of the ground-based photons and to duplicate it in their single photon onboard the satellite. The photons on the ground would have had their quantum state teleported to orbit. I think there is also a kind of encodings or encryptions of photonic states involved here.

Scientists noted that often people think of teleportation as transporting an actual object (or a photon) from one place to another like in the Star Trek. What we are transporting is *information* from one qubit (quantum bit) bit to another qubit. There is actually no physical transport of (physical) material but only information.

About five years ago, researchers could only transport quantum information, such as the direction a particle is spinning, across only a few meters. With the continuous and relentless progress and spirit in scientific experimentation and discovery, they can beam information across several miles across optical fibers (Dickerson, 2014) and now thousands of miles across space using lasers (Emspark, 2017).

Unlike the laser method, the optical fiber method could essentially be used to develop quantum technology but can only be used across very short distance. One good application of 'short-range quantum teleportation' would be in quantum computers so to effect extremely fast 'latency-free' computing, or even quantum cryptography that can make highly secure communications possible.

In all these scientific experiments as conducted in customized and precise laboratory setups, very special-purpose crystals, glass filters and prisms are used in perfect alignments as part of the transmitting or receiving modules and light splitting and recombining processes in addition with other semi-conductor components and glass fibers. What is to be greatly appreciated is quantum information are stored in some kind of crystals at both ends or multiple ends of the quantum teleportation network, and it is possible to imagine quantum entanglement is exploited within some kind of crystal-based data centers, the Alien kind! Yes, like the Alien Data Centers I am thinking of in this book. Very often and understandably so, enthusiasms of the quantum experiments need to appreciate the ultra-significant role of crystals than just focusing on getting scientific proofs.

Figure 11: Quantum Crystals - Crystals that can store quantum information using the power of quantum entanglement for teleporting information across extremely large distances breaking faster-than-light (FTL) limitations.

△ △ △

Quantum Computing

Traditional computing is based on manipulating and processing a binary language of 0s and 1s, basically like an alphanumeric set with just two characters or a sequence of subatomic particles arranged to represent either the north or south pole. Modern 21st century computers use this binary language by allowing or stopping the flow of electrical current through conducting metal and silicon circuits, altering the magnetic polarity or using some other mechanisms to affect a dual "on" or "off" state.

However, on the other hand, quantum computers use a very different language, one with an infinite number of "characters". If binary languages use the north and south poles of subatomic particles, then quantum computing would be using *all* possible points in between these two binary states.

Scientists have made the biggest and most complex quantum computer network yet to date, getting 20 different and entangled qubits (quantum bits) to 'communicate' with each other (Vance, 2018) i.e. a fully-controlled 20-qubit system. The team was able to read out the information contained in all those qubits. While past efforts have entangled larger groups of particles but in ultracold lasers, this is the first time researchers have been able to confirm this 'network of quantum computers' (quant-net) are indeed in a network of information-gathering collective.

Their work has pushed the boundaries of quantum computers to a new level, ever closer to the so-called "quantum advantage," where qubits out-perform the classical computation of binary bits based on silicon computers. While the team managed to entangle 20 particles together into a fully-controlled quantum network, though still not yet a true quantum computer but the largest such quantum network to date. It is after all a solid step towards the supercomputers of the future and ever closer to breaking the "quantum advantage" barrier. Some researchers said that a quantum computer is never going to replace classical computers but will add onto them. I think that Aliens have indeed broken the "quantum advantage" perhaps a billion times over and we are now just onto the early beginnings of understanding the incredible powers of crystals, proverbially scratching the surface of the super-crystal.

To recap, quantum entanglement happens when two subatomic particles stay connected no matter how far apart they are, and probably also independent of where in time the particles are. When one particle is 'disturbed', it instantly affects its entangled partner. It is impossible to tell the state of either particle until one is directly measured or 'read', but measuring one particle instantly determines the state of its partner. This is really cool!

△ △ △

Time Crystal: Infinite Source of Energy Through Time and Space

Crystals are infinitely amazing devices. They have truly spectacular properties that scientists are starting to research and discover more and more each day.

In a normal crystal, its arrangement of atoms regularly repeats itself in space. For example, the sodium and chloride ions in a salt crystal alternate in their spatial positions within the crystal. Crystals repeat in space, they grow larger in some shape and form over time.

One particular discovery of a new kind of crystal is called a Time Crystal. These new crystals have an atomic structure that allows them to repeat not just in space but also in time. What this means is that crystals can be a state of constant oscillation without energy (Macdonald, 2017).

Time Crystals were first predicted by Nobel-Prize winning physicist Frank Wilczek in 2012 (Wilczek, 2012), where time crystals are structures that appear to have movement even at their lowest energy state known as a ground state. Usually when a material is in ground state, also known as the zero-point energy of a system, it means subatomical movements should theoretically be impossible because that would require the crystal to expend energy (which is not possible because there is no energy available to expend). Wilczek predicted that time crystals do not belong to this category.

The atomic structures of normal crystals repeat in space, just like the normal carbon lattice of a diamond crystal. And just like a ruby or a diamond, they are motionless because they are all in equilibrium in their ground state. An easy way to imagine this is the case of jelly. When you give a tap on some jelly, it will jiggle repeatedly. The same phenomenon happens in time crystals, the big difference is that the motion occurs without any energy i.e. the crystal is not 'tapped'.

A time crystal is like the constantly oscillating jelly in its natural ground state, incapable of remaining still. This interesting feature is what makes time crystals a new phase of matter i.e. non-equilibrium matter.

These bizarre crystals, Time Crystals, can actually be made, be created. Scientists have confirmed an entirely new phase of matter. It has been predicted that there are many more strange and unknown types of matter out there in the universe that aren't in equilibrium (equilibrium matters are, for example, metals and insulators). These non-equilibrium matter could lead to breakthroughs in our understanding and deeper appreciation of the ancient world around us and in fact also of the ancient universe we live in. It could also encourage us to appreciate how Ancient Aliens might have used an architecture of quantum computing capabilities based on crystals, or perhaps new forms of massively-densed crystal super-structure computing.

Time Crystals rely on a quantum property called spin, which makes some atomic nuclei seem to 'spin' like a top. In the time crystals, the direction of that spin flipped at regular intervals of time or, in other words, frequency. Repeated radio waves pulses are used to trigger the flip-flopping of their spins. The interesting thing is that regardless of the imperfection of the radio-wave trigger, two newly discovered time crystals kept up a regular patter of flipping, revealing that they have a preferred time structure! What are these two newly discovered time-crystals and how are they made?

It is one thing to theorize the existence of time crystals and it is another to make them. In 2016, Yao (Yao, Potter, Potirniche, & Vishwanath, 2017) and his team came with a detailed blueprint that shows exactly how to make and measure the properties of a time crystal and even predict what the various phases surrounding the time crystals will be in – what this means is that we can now map out this new phase of matter i.e. *time*, like the equivalent of solid, liquid and gas phases. This is real science! Based on Yao's blueprint, two independent teams – one from the University of Maryland and one from Harvard – followed the steps and created their own time crystals later that year.

The Harvard Time Crystal (Choi, et al., 2017) was made with defects in a diamond crystal while the Maryland Time Crystal (Zhang, et al., 2017) used a chain of ions (electrically charged atoms) of the chemical element ytterbium.

Recently, researchers have two more types of materials exhibiting time-crystal capabilities, doubling the number of known time crystal habitats (Conover, 2018). The first of the two new time crystals, the Yale Time Crystal, was created by a team of scientists in a solid material called mono-ammonium phosphate (Rovny, Blum, & Barrett, 2018). Another team created its time crystal in a type of liquid containing star-shaped molecules (Pal, Nishad, Mahesh, & Sreejith, 2018).

The key is to excite the ions in the structure to keep them out of equilibrium. To do that, researchers alternately light up the crystals with two lasers. One laser to create the magnetic field and the second one to partially flip the spins of the atoms. Because the spins of all the atoms were entangled, the atoms settled into a stable, repetitive pattern of flipping their spins. The key word here is 'settled' which means an equilibrium and normal state for crystals. To become a time crystal, we need to break the time symmetry of the crystal. The two lasers that were periodically exciting the ytterbium atoms were producing a repetition in the system at twice the period of the laser excitations, this is something that could not happen in a normal system.

Coming to the jelly example, wouldn't it be weird the jelly somehow responds at a different period? Yes, it certainly would. The essence of time crystals is such that, when they are excited by a period laser driver at a period of T, the system somehow synchronizes so that when we observe the system, it is now oscillating with a period that is larger than T. Under different conditions of magnetic fields and laser pulsing, the time crystal would change phase, something like an ice cube melting.

A special note of the previously-mentioned new time crystal called mono-ammonium phosphate is that this time-crystal was created in a solid material with an orderly physical structure, yes, just like a traditional crystal! The other materials were disordered in structure. These discoveries – ability to break time symmetry of the crystal - are so new that scientists still aren't sure what more materials time crystals can be found in or what new ones to create. What this opens up is that time crystals could theoretically be created in many other forms of crystalline structures including ordinary crystals.

$$\triangle \ \triangle \ \triangle$$

Commanding Light of Crystals: Solid-State Lasers

It was recorded that René Descartes had seen light separated into the colors of the rainbow by glass or water. In 1666, Isaac Newton experimented on bending white light through a crystal-based prism to demonstrate that all colors already existed in the light, and that different colors fan out and travel with different speeds through the prism. Newton did not stop there. He also used a lens and a second prism to recompose the spectrum back into white light. Newton's experiment has become a classic example of the kind of 'scientific' methodology introduced during the scientific revolution. The results of the experiment transformed the field of metaphysics. Metaphysics is the branch of philosophy into the study of being, becoming, life, reality and existence. There is a lot more to write about the accomplishments and thinking of Newton and I shall leave it to another day perhaps. Now, what is quite clear about the works of Descartes and Newton, two of the world's great scientists and philosophers, is that it has somehow come together to maybe point out the possibilities which Aliens have mastered eons ago which is to actually have realized the metaphysical plane and perhaps mastering the realms of existence itself.

One common factor, I keep coming back to, is the significance around *Light* and around the *mastery of Light* and *Lasers* (high-powered light guided by crystal optics), and the applications of crystal-based technology.

A laser is a device that emits light through a process of optical amplification which is based on the stimulated emission of electromagnetic radiation. The team "laser" originated as an acronym for "light amplification by stimulated emission of radiation". A laser differs from other light sources in the way it emits light with properties of spatial and temporary coherence. There are applications of lasers and there are many types and operating principles of lasers that enable those applications. Lasers are used in many household appliances and computers like laser printers, optical disk drives like CDs, DVDs and Blu-ray, DNA sequencing instruments, fiber-optics and free-space optical communication, laser-surgery; for military and law enforcement, and medical. In the previous sections, we have also seen lasers being used in quantum-based experiments.

Well, there are many types of lasers such as gas lasers, chemical lasers, Excimer lasers, etc. The one particular type of laser of which I am particularly interested in is the solid-state laser. Solid-state lasers have been the center piece of quantum entanglement experiments.

A solid-state laser is a laser that uses a gain medium that is a solid rather a liquid or gas. The "gain medium" is also known as the "active laser medium". It is the source of optical gain within a laser. Examples of "gain medium" include certain crystals, typically doped with rare-earth ions (e.g. neodymium, ytterbium or erbium) or transition metal ions (e.g. titanium or chromium); most often yttrium aluminum garnet ($Y_3Al_5O_{12}$), yttrium orthovanadate (YVO_4), or sapphire (AL_2O_3).

Figure 12: Nd:YVO4 - Neodymium-Doped Yttrium Vanadate crystal shows excellence in efficiency, physical, optical and mechanical properties for wide applications as laser material for diode-pumped solid-state (DPSS) lasers to yield stable and powerful red, green and infrared lasers.

In order to fire a laser, the active laser medium must be in a non-thermal energy distribution state known as a population inversion (occurs when a system exists in a state where there are more members of the system in higher excited states than in lower unexcited states). To be in a state of population inversion, an external energy source is required, which is called laser pumping. Laser pumping is mostly achieved with electrical currents or with light generated by other lasers. More exotic gain media can be pumped by chemical reactions (think magma-based crystal caves), nuclear fission or with high-energy electron beams.

Generally, the "gain medium" of a solid-state laser consists of a glass or crystalline "host" material, to which is added a "dopant[5]" such as neodymium, chromium, erbium, thulium or ytterbium, all of which are rare-earth elements, to get the base or host crystal to provide the required energy states. The most commonly-used solid-state gain media is neodymium-doped yttrium aluminate garnet (Nd:YAG). To activate lasers with very high power levels in the terawatt range and high energies

---

[5] A dopant is a trace impurity that is inserted into a "host" substance, often in low concentrations, to modify the electrical or optical properties of the host substance. In the case of crystalline substances, the atoms of the dopant very commonly take the place of elements that were in the crystal lattice of the base material.

(megajoules), neodymium-doped glass (Nd: glass) and ytterbium-doped glass or ceramics are used. It is interesting to note that the first material used for lasers was synthetic ruby crystals but they are not common laser applications because of their lower power efficiencies.

New solid-state laser systems outputs about 40% of available energy into its beam, which is considered very high for solid-state lasers. A strong electrical setup as a power source, like in modern hybrid engine and propulsion systems, would most likely be required to power such solid-state laser systems.

The use of super-powered light, lasers to be precise, to harness and extend the quantum realm and the use of crystals to realize the super properties of quantum mechanics truly belong to realms of super advanced Alien technology.

△ △ △

Ultra-High Memory Crystals

Scientists have invented a new data storage medium that is based on crystals. Lasers are used to encode data and information on these crystals. The crystals are so good at storing data that they could survive longer for billions of years, provided they are not intentionally destroyed. Crystal devices can store data in multiple dimensions.

One recently created crystal storage device is able to store data in five dimensions including the standard three dimensions of space but also two extra dimensions within its crystal lattice. The "Ultra-High Memory Crystal" is a real and futuristic storage device with unprecedented features which includes a 360 Terabyte (TB) per crystal 'disc' data capacity (about 500,000 CDs), thermal stability upwards of 1000s of degree centigrade and a practically unlimited lifetime as like crystals.

In our reference to Superman in previous chapters, he used a "Primary Crystal Key" to *create* his "Fortress of Solitude". Superman has also been using all kinds of crystals, including inserting his "Primary Crystal Key" into a crystal receptor to interface with the crystal-based console. See Figure 8. Well, now it appears that sci-fi has now become a scientific reality.

Incidentally, the motivation to invent memory crystals was to solve the data archiving problem faced by museums, libraries, and today's data centers. Currently large archives of data have to be backed up to new hard drives every five to ten years because the lifespan of hard drives is relatively short at 100 years.

How is the "Ultra-High Memory Crystal" made? The data is encoded by shooting ultra-fast lasers into a crystal lattice via self-assembled nanostructures created in fused quartz which is able to store tremendous quantities of data for billions of years (Kazansky, et al., 2016). When the data-encoding femtosecond laser marks the glass, it makes a pit with a nanograting. This nanograting produces birefringence that is characterized by two additional optical parameters or dimensions. The information encoding is realized in five dimensions, which include the two optical dimensions (the slow-axis orientation as the fourth dimension, and the strength of retardance – defined as a product of the birefringence and the length of the structure – forms the fifth dimension), in addition to the three spatial dimensions of these nanostructures in the crystal. The parameters of the two above-mentioned optical dimensions are controlled during encoding by the polarization and light intensity, respectively. Thus, by using these two additional optical dimensions to the three spatial dimensions, the 5D ultra-high memory crystal storage medium is realized.

By using ultra-fast lasers, we can now 'etch' or encode data and information into a piece of quartz with 5D information in the form of nanostructured dots separated by only one millionth of a meter or possibly even much lesser- see Figure 13. The self-assembled nanostructures change the way light travels through the glass crystal, thus changing the polarization of the light. The data encoded there can then be read by the light received, via a combination of optical microscope and a polarizer.

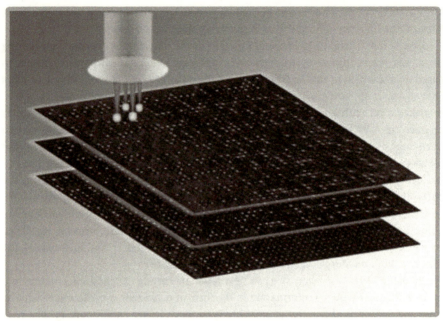

Figure 13: Memory Crystal - Digital data encoded into 5D optical data storage. Designed to store upwards of 360TB of data on a single slice of crystal glass.

The first digital documents - the Universal Declaration of Human Rights, Newton's Opticks, the Magna Carta and the King James Bible - have been recorded onto a "Ultra-High Memory Crystal" across 18 layers using optimized parameters (light pulses with energies of 0.2µJ and a duration of 600fs at a repetition rate of 500kHz). The durability of the storage medium was tested by using accelerated aging measurements. The tests revealed the decay time of the nanogratings is $3 \times 10^{20\pm1}$ years at room temperature (30°C or 303K), showing the extremely high stability of nanostructures imprinted in fused quartz. Even at elevated temperatures of 189°C (462K), the extrapolated decay time is comparable to the current age of the Universe (13.8 billion years or 1.38×10^9 years). Another way of thinking about it is these copies of memory crystals could survive the life of most planets or stars or probably even the human race.

How can we scale up the storage density of the crystal or enable the reading of data stored in these memory crystals or the faster writing of data into the memory crystals? The addition of more states of polarization and intensities – currently limited by the resolutions of the slow-axis orientation (4.7°) and the retardance (5nm) - could enable more than one byte per modification spot using the same birefringence system, thus more storage capacity.

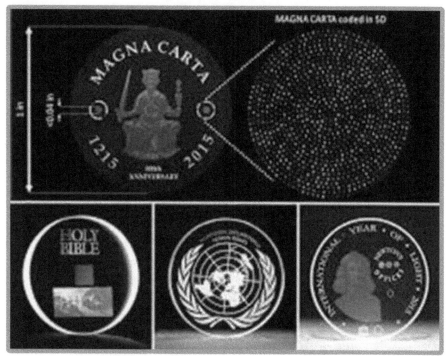

Figure 14:   Ultra-High Memory Crystal - New 5D memory storage in glass crystal: the Magna Carta (top), King James Bible (bottom left), the Universal Declaration of Human Rights (bottom center), Newton's Opticks (right).

What this means is that this kind of technology that manipulates the five dimensions in a crystal lattice can help secure the evidence of an evolving civilization or even record the history of the last one so that all the wisdom and knowledge we have learnt or information we have collected will never be forgotten but will ever be ready to be passed on. This property of "information immortality" is one remarkable feature set enabled by the clever manipulation of crystal-based technology. More so, this technology is key to the eternal storage and manipulation of data processing and computation in Alien Data Centers, including those on Earth and also on nearby planets or elsewhere in the Cosmos.

I think similar technologies can be used to create other forms of crystal memory storage structures that can mimic the different kinds of memory storage we use today in our computer systems and microcontrollers such as those for smart cars and other smart electronic devices. I am thinking RAM (Random Access Memory), EEPROM (Electrically Erasable Programmable Read-Only Memory) etc. To enable the implementation of the end-to-end "Universal Solution Architecture" of Aliens we would need much more crystal devices. I will most able to continue this thread of new discovery and theories in my next book.

There is a new speculation that time crystals could potentially be used as a source of infinite energy to power some kind of perpetual crystal computing devices which in turn would power up these Alien Data Centers indefinitely. Another awesome thing to note is that time crystals were created in an entangled state! The reality of coupling the properties of non-equilibrium matter and unlimited energy source with quantum entanglement to create new forms of super crystals is certainly getting increasingly exciting. But not for the Aliens who probably have long mastered the science of these crystal-based technologies and have been creating bases of Alien Data Centers out of them.

The *General Theory of Aliens* is that the key components essential to the building of Alien Data Centers is based on manipulating the structure of super crystals and its super properties. To be specific to the point, we need crystals that can function in myriad of capabilities to provide high-density storage, super-computing and information processing, super high-speed information sharing which means ultra-high-speed networking bandwidths etc. I believe Alien Data Centers are built upon a foundation of crystal-based infrastructure, of crystal-based intelligent computing equipment and devices of the examples I have described in this chapter.

In the next chapter, I will talk about my theory about the Unidentified Flying Object (UFO) phenomenon. UFOs is a world-wide mysterious phenomenon with millions of sightings every year, thousands a day, all over the world, across all cultures. Let's go ...

"Crystal caves in Axiom:Heart, a beautiful Kingdom of Light with motionless motion."

6

UFOs of Crystals and Light

✳

"NOT much use are Jyu-n's hands, entering a meditative stance seeking guidance from Peng*Xen, the 'All-Seeing Mind'."

IN EVERY DIRECTION, MULTI-COLORED OPTICAL LIGHTS ARE SHINING IN BEAUTIFULLY INDECPHIRABLE PATTERNS OF EVER-VARYING INTENSITY AND FREQUENCIES. Lights moving in inexplicable patterns and with amazing exhilarating speeds, wild accelerations and instant stoppings. There are lights everywhere, everyone standing, all breathless.

What are all these lights? Why are they here? What purposes do they serve? What special meaning can there be so we can understand? What can we learn from them?

△ △ △

Unidentified Flying Objects: UFOs

An unidentified flying object (UFO) is an object observed in the sky that is not readily identified by sight or instruments. Most UFOs are later identified as conventional flying objects or some natural phenomenon. The term of UFO is also widely used for claimed observations of extraterrestrial spacecraft. The latter phenomenon is very often the more interesting speculation of all time.

The term "UFO" was coined in 1953 by the United Air Force (USAF) to be the general category to classify all reports of flying objects that can't be identified. During the late 1940s and through the 1950s, "flying saucers" or "flying disks" were often attributed as UFOs. Various studies have so far concluded the UFO phenomenon does not represent a threat to national security, which gathered considerable interest during the Cold War, nor does it contain anything worthy of scientific pursuit. But more recently in the 2010s, the interest in UFOs gained momentum. In popular usages, the term UFO became synonymous with the phenomenon of alien spacecrafts.

Various studies have established that the majority of UFO observations are mis-identified conventional objects or even natural phenomenon such as aircraft, balloons, noctilucent clouds, nacreous clouds or astronomical objects such as meteors or bright planets. Between 5 to 20% of reported sightings are not explained and therefore, in the strictest sense, can be classified as true UFOs. The proponents of the Extraterrestrial Hypothesis (ETH) suggest that these unexplained reports are of alien spacecraft. In addition, the usage of the *Null Hypothesis* to attributing the unexplained UFO phenomenon to the instances of alien spacecraft is that the theory is assumed true until evidence proves otherwise, at least to a statistically significant degree.

Now, the concept of a null hypothesis is used differently in two approaches to statistical inference. In the significance testing approach, a null hypothesis is rejected if the observed data are significantly unlikely to have occurred if the null hypothesis were true. In this case, the null hypothesis is rejected and an alternative hypothesis is tested in its place. If the data are consistent with the null hypothesis, it is not rejected. This is analogous to the legal principle of presumption of innocence, in which a suspect or defendant is assumed to be innocent (null is not rejected) until proven guilty (null is rejected) beyond a reasonable doubt (to a statistically significant degree).

Unexplained aviation and aerospace observations have been reported throughout history, across the world by most if not all cultures. Some observations were undoubtedly astronomical in nature such as meteors, comets, planets that be seen with the naked but untrained eye, or atmospheric optical phenomenon such as parhelia and lenticular clouds, or even optical illusions. An example is Halley's Comet which was first recorded by Chinese astronomers in 240 BCE and possibly as early as 467 BCE.

*What particularly interests me is the so called the phenomenon of optical illusions. Actually, yes, I believe UFOs **are** indeed optical illusions but with a bit of clever alien twist. What could cause optical illusions?*

Experts suggest the mysterious sky sightings of UFOs are better explained by optical illusions like "green flashes", "inversion", and "ghost" mirages than actual alien spacecrafts. These so-called types of optical illusions have tormented aircraft pilots and keen air passengers for decades. These illusions are believed to be created by the different layers of air acting like giant lenses with the Sun as the light source. The physics behind the observations of these optical effects can be demonstrated by the eye, cameras, and video recordings. For example, a "secondary sun" is a remarkably bright solar reflection from layers of ice crystals suspending in the air. The reflection's circular or flattened shape could resemble a UFO shaped like, for example, a circular flying disk doing a steep banking maneuver. I have listed the 12 most common shapes of UFOs in Table 1 on page 79. Expert photographers will attribute "green spots" or "green flashes" as "ghosts" – an internal reflection in the camera lens itself. See Figure 15 for an example for this "ghost" effect. In this case, it is caused by the broadband anti-reflection coatings used on the Canon lens which were designed to minimize reflections across a wide spectrum by reducing them to the lowest possible value in the red and blue. However, the side effect of this method leaves a little reflection in the middle of the spectrum, that is, in the green. This method will work if the residual reflection is weak. But when photographing sunsets, especially where the Sun is too over-exposed, the green reflection becomes visible. Internal reflections are more common in zoom lenses because their large number of lens elements and surfaces create more opportunities for reflections to occur.

"Green ghosts" like this are typically captured in images at a position diametrically opposite to the over-exposed Sun. In Figure 15, the Sun is to the upper right of center, and the ghost is to the lower left. This green reflection, about the center of the image superimposed on the dark side of a ridge, is an apparent giveaway that the spurious image is a ghost and therefore not a UFO. Or is it?

Figure 15:   "Green Patch" - On the horizon just to the left of center under the over-exposed sun during a phase of the sunset. Image taken with a 6× zoom lens of a Canon G9.

Smartphones with multiple CMOS cameras and digital cameras are very common these days. There are over two billion smartphones on the planet. A common feature is automatic adjustment of color balance. Most digital cameras look at the relative levels of the primary colors in the scene and then try to adjust the color to make the image look 'right'. For example, if we take a picture in open shade, where the illumination comes from the blue sky, the camera reduces the brightness of the blue sub-image and increases the gain for the red, so that objects in the image come out close to their "correct" colors. Similarly, if we take a picture indoors with incandescent light, the camera compensates for the reddish hue by boosting the blue and reducing the red content of the image. Our eyes do all this automatically while cameras provide the advantage of compensation for the lighting automatically.

Another artifact of digital cameras is due to charge spill in their CCD detectors. What we see in Figure 16 is due to the leakage along the columns of the CCD detector in the camera, caused by the over-exposed solar image. This is a camera artifact, what the camera manufacturer calls a feature, not an atmospheric phenomenon and not a UFO-related phenomenon. Or is it?

Figure 16: "Green Streak" - Captured by a digital camera, caused by a leakage along the columns of the CCD detector in the camera.

The key word here is **optical**. Aliens have perfected their applications of crystal-based technologies and science, and in this case to their spacecrafts and spaceflight. I believe Aliens have been taking great advantage of the effects of "optical illusions" to disguise and optically camouflage their spacecrafts and in turn to mask their flight-paths from unwarranted tracking. I believe Aliens have always been fooling our digital cameras into capturing nothing but camera artifacts instead of their spacecrafts. They have made use of the knowledge of 'defects' in our camera technology to 'cover up' their true presence. It is true that our eyes may not be fooled by what we see but when we tried to take a picture of the UFO as evidence, viola, the pictures become the defective "green flashes" and "green spots" in those pictures – where evidence were 'mysteriously' transformed into defective images and no more proof. What a clever way Aliens are using to mask their presence from us (evidence hunters)!

△ △ △

Into Formation

The word *crystal* is derived from the Ancient Greek word κρύσταλλος (*krustallos*) meaning both "ice" and "rock crystal", from κρύος (*kruos*), "icy cold, frost".

A crystal or crystalline solid is a solid material whose constituents – atoms, molecules or ions – are arranged in a highly-ordered *microscopic* structure to form a lattice of crystal that extends in all directions. Additionally, *macroscopic* single crystals are usually identifiable by their geometrical shape, usually consisting of flat faces with specific and characteristic orientations. The process of forming crystals via mechanisms of crystal growth is called crystallization or solidification. An example of a crystal, the Selenite "Sword" crystal, can be seen in Figure 4 on page 29.

Examples of crystals include snowflakes, diamonds and table salt. Most inorganic solids are not crystals but polycrystals, which are many microscopic crystals fused together into a single solid. Examples of polycrystals include most metals, rocks, ceramics and ice. A third category of solids is amorphous solids, where the atoms have no periodic structure. Examples of amorphous solids include glass, wax, and many plastics.

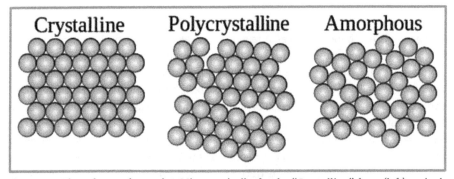

Figure 17:   Three forms of crystals - Microscopically, for the "Crystalline" form (left), a single crystal is made up of atoms in a perfect periodic arrangement and with no defects and no grain boundaries; for the "Polycrystalline" form (center), a polycrystal is composed of many microscopic crystals (called "crystallites" or "grains"); and in "Amorphous" form (right), the amorphous or non-crystalline solid has no periodic arrangements nor long-range order that is characteristic of a crystal even microscopically such as glass, polymers and gels.

Crystals are commonly recognized by their shapes, the number of flat faces and sharp corners. The flat faces, also called facets, are oriented in a specific way in relation to its underlying base atomic arrangement of the crystal. As a crystal grows, new atoms attach more easily to the rougher and less stable parts of the surface, and less easily to the flat stable surfaces. In this way, these parts of the crystal grow very quickly, the flat surfaces tend to grow larger and smoother until the whole crystal surface consists of these plane surfaces.

The external shape or form of a crystal is called a crystal's habit. This is determined by the crystal structure – which restricts the possible facet orientations, the specific crystal chemistry and bonding, and the conditions under which the crystal is formed. Crystals can grow to as large a size as they possibly can within the special environment they grow in. See "Cave of Crystals" in Section "Super Giant Crystal Caves" on page 26, where still-growing giant crystal beams are found to be thriving.

Crystallization is the process of forming a crystalline structure either from a fluid or from materials dissolved in a fluid. Crystallization is a complex and extensively-studied field because, depending on the conditions, a single fluid can solidify into many possible forms. It can create a single crystal – perhaps with many possible phases, impurities, stoichiometries[6], defects and habits. Or, it can become a polycrystal with many possibilities for the size, arrangement, orientation and phase of its grains. The final form of the solid is determined by the conditions in which the fluid is solidifying from, such as the chemistry of the fluid, the ambient pressure and the temperature, and the speed with which all the parameters of crystal-growing are changing.

An *ideal* crystal has every atom or molecule in a perfect and exact repeating pattern. However, in reality, most crystalline materials have a variety of crystallographic defects i.e. places where the crystal's patterns are disrupted. Clearly, the types and structures of these defects may have a characteristic effect on the properties of the crystal. A few examples of crystallographic defects include vacancy defects – an empty space where an atom should be in the lattice, interstitial defects – an extra atom squeezed in where it does not fit, and dislocations – edge dislocations and screw dislocations. Impurity is another common type of crystallographic defect, which means the 'wrong' type of atom is instead present in a crystal.

A *perfect* diamond crystal would only contain carbon atoms, and a *real* diamond crystal might also perhaps contain a few boron atoms. These boron impurities change the diamond's color to a slightly blue hue. Similar, the only difference between ruby and sapphire is the presence of impurities in a corundum (transparent crystalline form of aluminum oxide, typically containing traces of iron, titanium, vanadium and

---

[6] Stoichiometries is the calculation of reactants and products in chemical reactions.

chromium) crystal. A dopant is a special type of impurity used in semi-conductors to change the crystal's electrical properties, often used as the gain medium to create solid-state lasers for quantum experiments. Other types of impurities can be due to a phenomenon called *twinning* (a twin boundary has different crystal orientations on its two sides not in a random but specific mirror-image way); and *mosaicity* (a spread of crystal plane orientations resulting in the mosaic crystal containing smaller crystalline units somehow misaligned with respect to each other).

Crystals have certain special electrical, optical and mechanical properties that glass and polycrystals normally do not have. These properties are linked to the anisotropy of the crystal, i.e. due to the lack of rotational symmetry in its atomic arrangement. One important such property is the *piezoelectric effect*, where a voltage across the crystal can augment its dimensions i.e. stretch or shrink it. Or, inversely, where a mechanical force or stress when applied to the crystal produces an electrical current within the crystal. Another property is *birefringence* which I have covered in Section "Ultra-High Memory Crystals" on page 56, a unique feature used in the production of ultra-high memory storage media. As I have also written in the Chapter "Incredible Powers of Crystals" starting on page 43, crystals are used in various applications like solid-state lasers, ultra-high memory storage media, and storage of entangled quantum photons being one of the most interesting usages of the magnificent crystal.

As a matter of fact, large single crystals have been created by geological processes. The immense variety of rocks and minerals can be found all over and within our planet. Ever since the formation of Earth over four billion years ago, various planetary-wide geological processes have been in play ever since, forging the plethora of natural elements, be it native or alien, into unique crystalline formations and structures.

As we have seen in the Section "Super Giant Crystal Caves" on page 26, selenite crystal beams in excess of 10 meters are found in the "Cave of Crystals" in Naica, Mexico. Interestingly, biological processes can also form crystals, for example calcite and aragonite in this case by most molluscs (slugs, snails, oysters, clams, octopuses and cuttlefish) or hydroxylapatite in the case of vertebrates. Some organisms have special techniques to *prevent* crystallization from occurring such as antifreeze proteins (AFPs), produced by certain vertebrates, plants, fungi and bacteria that permit their survival in subzero environments.

Although there are more than 4,000 officially recognized and recorded mineral species, unsurprisingly, some are found to have detrimental often damaging effects on organic life, that is despite how beautiful they can *appear* to be, they are dangerous. For example, the green crystals, Torbernite, are made of uranium and found within granite. Due to its natural beauty, with Torbernite the prize coveted among crystal and mineral collectors, careful handling and storage are paramount. As these green crystals are not only radioactive, they release deadly radon gas if heated.

Figure 18: Torbernite - Radioactive Green Crystals. Special handling and storage required, will release deadly radon gas if heated.

Chalcanthite is another example of dangerous crystals. When broken down and introduced to water, the beautiful blue Chalcanthite crystals are capable of shutting down the vital survival functions of fish and plant life. This crystal has traditionally been used to clear ponds of undesirable plant or algae growth.

Figure 19:   Chalcanthite - Blue crystals toxic to fish and aquatic plant life.

Back to UFOs, I think Aliens have been using another kind of optical illusions other than reflections, intentional over-exposing or saturation of camera detectors.

What if Aliens were able to turn their spacecraft invisible or transparent to incident light, or only reflecting a certain color of light, whether it is operating in the day, night or in wet weather conditions, basically in all weather conditions?

△ △ △

Invisibility

Scientists, at the Air Force Research Laboratory of the Wright-Patterson Air Force Base in Ohio, have created a new liquid crystal that can reflect different colors of light with increasing applied voltages, thus transitioning from mostly transparent to almost mirror-like properties. This idea of a tunable mirror has led to smart windows that can block heat in the summer or let heat pass through in the winter, or provide a way to toggle the opacity of a screen between an indoor and outdoor setting (Lee, et al., 2014).

The mirror was made of materials called cholesteric liquid crystals (CLCs). These liquid crystals are made of molecules that arrange themselves into a helical structure. The range of wavelengths the CLC material reflect, usually a narrow range of about 50 to 100nm, is a function of the distance between molecules in the crystal. Voltages were applied to broaden this reflection wavelength range to about 600nm, wider than the visible spectrum. This means that the liquid crystals reflected enough wavelengths that they became like mirrors.

It was not difficult to make mirror CLCs. They were made with commercially available components already used to make liquid crystals. A combination of a liquid-crystal diacrylate monomer – dopants that make crystals with a right- or left-handed twist, and a mixture of components that serve as a host to keep the liquid-crystal molecules in the helical structure. The molecules in a typical liquid-crystal with a different type of host could shift their positions when an electric current is applied. To prevent this, a small amount of photoinitiator was added to the mixture and the material polymerized with ultraviolet light. The center point of the wavelengths reflected is governed by the amount of temperature used to polymerized the CLCs.

As a CLC will only reflect light with a polarization that matches the orientation of the helices i.e. the handedness, a right- and a left-handed crystal were made and then stacked together so as to reflect all incoming light.

As an increasing amount of voltage was applied to the device, the reflected wavelengths expanded symmetrically around the center wavelength, thus altering the color returned to the observer. It was hypothesized that turning up the voltage physically stretched the polymer network of the material, widening the gap between the molecules in the helical structure. To transit from almost transparent to mirror-like took an 80V increase. The switching speed of this CLC is very slow compared to standard liquid crystals used in some displays – about 25 seconds to turn any level of reflection and about 10 seconds to switch it off. It was found that applying an extra

15V or 30V burst for about a second to prime the material can speed up the performance to about two seconds. This would be fast enough to control the spectral properties of a smart surface from transmissive to reflective. The bottom-right image of Figure 20 shows the almost-silver mirror-effect of the CLC where all wavelengths had been reflected (except for the ultraviolet spectrum).

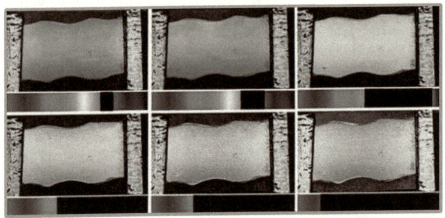

Figure 20: A Tunable Liquid-Crystal Mirror - Increasing voltages rising from 0V (top left) to 15, 30, 60, 90 and 110V (bottom right) applied to the CLC reflects an increasing range of colors. Black bar at bottom of each image indicates which part of the light spectrum was reflected. (Lee, et al., 2014)

How would Aliens utilize this special kind of reflection-control properties of crystals? I think their spacecrafts were somehow coated or wrapped in layers of this kind of crystalline materials. Automatic controls within, or perhaps external to the spacecraft, would dynamically adjust the amount of wavelength reflections to fool all photographical captures by spying cameras. To further that thought, I think alien spacecrafts could actually be entirely made of crystals. We have seen how crystals can be grow by natural geological forces. Perhaps Aliens were able to grow their spacecrafts from crystals in any specifications they desire, perhaps able to control its geometries and forms, its computing and processing capabilities, and its high-energy crystal-powered laser weapons, by manipulating crystals at the atomic level. With their technology to build controls based on the properties of quantum entanglement, it could even be possible that Aliens were remotely controlling their spacecrafts from far away with no latency at all i.e. similar to what we do today with the Unmanned Aviation Vehicles (UAVs) or aerial drones. This could herald a new UFO phenomenon which I call "Unmanned UFO" (UUFO).

An Alien spacecraft made out of crystals could also explain why it is so difficult to find or 'retrieve' any credible evidence of spacecraft remnants at possible crash sites, simply because there is nothing significantly left there to find, nothing discrete enough to be called out. The Alien spacecrafts would have broken up and shattered with great forces into a billion crystalline pieces upon high impacts at great velocities. Perhaps, these crystal-bearing spacecrafts are designed as redundant structures in function meant to be disposable when their use has been met. To protect the precious cargo that it is transporting from falling into the wrong hands or losing its secrets to undesirable elements, the alien spacecraft could have been remotely activated to self-destruct or activated by its pilots. The resulting crystalline pieces would be indistinguishable from ordinary shards of glass on any geological landscape, mountains or in the oceans.

△ △ △

UFOs: Information Transporters

On Earth, building a data center is not a trivial matter. It takes a lot of considerations and full-scale planning. Sections on "Internet Data Centers" and "Data Center Transformation: Inevitability" on pages 19 and 22 respectively provide good measures of efforts and concerns about them.

Let us assume for a while that we have a real crystal ball, the kind that allows us to look into the future, to observe and to learn about anything we want. What will we see?

For applications in today's data centers to operate and function properly as intended, there are many situations where professional couriers are used to transport physical storage devices like HDDs (Hard Disk Drives) or magnetic tapes from one data center (your organization for example) to another data center (could be your cloud provider). This service is called "Drive Shipping". Organizations who migrate their email inboxes to Office 365 (a Microsoft Office product) normally use "Drive Shipping" to bulk-import their PST files to user mailboxes in the cloud. "Drive Shipping" means that you manually copy the PST files into a hard disk drive (HDD) and then physically ship (usually you use a professional couriering company like DHL or UPS) the drive to

Microsoft. When Microsoft receive your hard drive, its data center personnel will copy the data from your hard drive to a storage area in the Microsoft cloud. Using "Drive Shipping" to import PST files to user mailboxes in the Cloud is one way to migrate your organization's email to Office 365 (which is cloud-based). The main reason for using "Drive Shipping" this way is to save a huge cost of transporting the data over the internet which can be very costly and highly time consuming, considering you will need a high-speed VPN link with potentially tens of Gbps bandwidth and with high encryption to secure the data payload during transmission.

Internet protocols like HTTPS, FTP, SFTP, SSH help companies transfer different kinds of data around the internet, either over a batch mode (usually activated in non-peak time periods to save costs) or in real-time mode. Depending on the application or costs, you can typically choose a particular suitable protocol that can meet your business or technical requirements. But file replication and off-site backup like data duplication schemes frequently deal with a very high volume of data that would take too long, be too costly and also be too risky when just using internet links and would quickly fill up the finite bandwidth or data quota.

The traditional parcel couriering still stands out as a simple and useful solution for moving bulk volumes of data. Who has time to drain a swimming pool with a straw or the patience for that?

Data transfer connections or intensive automatic data migration processes could time-out due to unresponsive servers or heavy workloads or unrecoverable data loss due to network congestion or a bad glitchy connection or suffer from badly configured DNS mappings. Data transfer over the internet could be prone to Man-In-The-Middle attacks, eavesdropping and perhaps intentional redirecting away from your intended destinations without the knowledge of your engineers.

For data duplication and backup strategies, many companies have turned to external sites as secondary storage areas. If we have implemented plenty of bandwidth and are storing modest amounts of data records or data sets, then it would be fine if we use one of the internet data transfer protocols, as mentioned above, to get our base data image to our cloud. Now, data to be duplicated or for backup purposes could include critical software images, bank records, government records, financial records, and basically any data that is deemed to be precious and priceless and would hurt a lot if gone missing, be irrecoverable, irretrievable or irreplaceable.

Regulatory standards or compliance can dictate the timely transmission of data with specific time periods for vital information to reach certain parties. In this instance, electronic data transfer with the best protocol is the way to go. If documents are smaller and there are no issues with network loads or speeds causing slow-downs or undesirable latencies to affect customer experience that comes with replicating the entire database, then "Drive Shipping" is not choice for data transfer.

For larger data sets, we usually demand answers to two best practices:

o   Which data transfer protocol will get data from one location to an off-site target server as fast and as secured as possible?

o   Can our local network handle the transfer of massive volumes of data and disk images without affecting users, customers and other applications running in the data center or company networks?

The architecture principle is never to hinder your local network or user and system connections to the cloud or SaaS application. The company needs to remain online ("always-on") and operate in the best interactive mode with the lowest latency to get all work done, with the best end-to-end user experience and always there to serve customers at all times during the day and night.

An important thing to note is to take precautions when shipping your data in a hard drive or any other physical device via couriers. The physical device could be damaged on transit, lost or stolen or delayed. Necessary steps must be taken to ensure the safety of the hard drives – encrypting the drives and data they are storing and also to ruggedize the form factor it is being transported in. A copy of the data must be kept at the source location while the seed drives are transported. Packages carrying the drives must be packed safely to protect them from shocks or hard handling or water immersion often encountered during transit. A tracking number and even a location tracking device using GPS can be used to insure the shipment and definitely to employ the services of a professional data courier or a tracker in the events of theft or loss.

Professional logistics and expert fleet management ensure timely and secure deliveries of data packages. Data courier vendors who are well-versed in transporting physical backup data help cloud vendors to quickly import data into the cloud data centers and to deliver quick service uptime for customers. In cases where the primary data center fails due to natural disaster, the backup data needs to be physically transported to another data center, usually located at least 50km away and within a few hours to be compliant with RPO (Recovery Point Objective) and RTO (Recovery Time Objective) times. This forms the "Disaster Recovery" best practice, enterprises need to adopt.

With general data transfer and data migration, the best practice is always to consider the context and limitations of all the methods at hand, carefully consider the advantages gained vs the disadvantages of each method, and then to make the best option possible that can satisfy the data transfer objective. These considerations, among others mentioned in previous chapters, will get that much more serious when the data payload is of high significant value and consists of highly-confidential information. It is all about the data! Harness the data to create valuable insights, create intelligence, *CREATE Life, CREATE Minds, CREATE Souls, PROLONG Existence, EXPAND Existence* ... The stakes are very high! Even for Aliens if I may add.

Now, what has any of these "Drive Shipping" and data center architecture best practices got to do with UFOs? What similarities can we learn from them?

I believe that UFOs are much more than what they are thought of, much more than just flying machines or "flying saucers". UFOs can be magnificent and beautiful flying machines, fitted with advanced navigational technologies and faster-than-light capabilities; have the ability to fool digital detections, to hide in plain sight and go invisible. In my opinion, UFOs are the 'workhorse' of the Alien civilization.

UFOs, like today's data cargo transporters or "drive shippers", are designed to transport items, adhering to strict secure protocols and proven patterns, from one location to another across the vast expanse of space (outer space) and time, basically from point to point in the Universe. As we have learned in previous chapters about the various super powers of crystals, in their computational capabilities and their important role in the operations of Alien Data Centers, I believe the UFOs are transporting the essential ingredients to creating minds, yes, Quantum Crystals.

The entire UFO could also be made of Quantum Crystals. Specifically, the UFO itself could actually be the very Quantum Computers the Alien Data Centers are running on. As we have also learned, data centers are built with many types of computer servers with specialized functionalities and structures. I believe that the shapes and functions of each type of UFOs will be different depending on the specific purposes or their roles with regards to the operations of the Alien Data Centers that are co-located on Planet Earth of the Milky Way Galaxy.

One important design feature of data centers is 'Modularity and Flexibility'. Most would think UFOs may have singular purposes. What if I turn it around and propose that UFOs are actually built as modules that can be assembled into new shapes and functions, and are ready to 'dock' into the Alien data center at the location they are designed for? When a computer subsystem such as a server unit becomes non-optimal or damaged or malfunctioned, the data center engineer would order a new part or retrieve one from its store, swap out the damaged unit and swap in the new one. All this is done without any perceivable down-time at all. These "hot-swappable" components are designed to be modular components to ensure ease of replacement with the sole goal of keeping everything running smoothly as they should be and with the most minimal of disruptions to the operations of the data center. Alien Data Center Architects had specially designed each UFO type as modules that would assemble together and fit into other UFOs to form new data center functions according to a higher pre-programed function or directive.

The form of the UFO would follow its function. There is a Design *Law* of "Form follows Function", often associated with modernist architecture and industrial design which says that the shape of a building or object should primarily be designed to accentuate its intended function or purpose. "Form" and "Function" are two different things. The "Form" is about the structure, the shape of a building, an object, or a device; whereas the "Function" is the purpose of the structure or its role. Additionally, "Form follows Function" is a principle that the shape (*form*) that something takes should be chosen based on the intended purpose and its *function*. This principle is often applied to works of civil architecture, engineering, handset design, product design, graphic design, user interface, vehicles, military jets and many more.

Over the years since ancient times, there have been many sightings of UFOs, dating back to a few centuries B.C. According to The National UFO Reporting Center Online Database (NUFORC), there have been more than 80,000 reports of strange objects in the sky since 7 July 1947, where a "flying disc" containing extra-terrestrial lifeform was reported to have crashed at a ranch about 30 miles north of Roswell in New Mexico, USA. The NUFORC dataset provides much more details on individual sightings of which the most significant feature of each report is the shape of the object, besides its time and location. The NUFORC dataset classifies about 46 possible shapes of which several overlap each other. For a more productive representation and analysis, I will provide 12 most common shapes.

Over the past eight decades, there have been many reports of UFOs with various different shapes. In many of the UFO reports, some of the shapes could not be clearly described or shapes that might easily be viewed as man-made.

Identifying unidentified flying objects is a difficult task especially the object to be identified happens to be flying in irregular and unpredictable movements and maneuvers, and very often at super high speeds and from unknown directions. By the time the observers' attention was fixed at the UFOs, most of the latter's earlier maneuvers were already missed, noting only the last few short moments of their movements. Figure 21 shows the most common observations of UFOs' movements and maneuvers recorded so far.

I think I have a possible explanation to these UFO movements. Alien spacecrafts are actually communicating and signaling with the "custodians" of the Alien Data Centers via aerial movements of their spacecrafts. UFO movements can be interpreted as some kind of an accepted or standardized communication handshake between the two parties, perhaps to "authenticate" and request permission to enter the Alien Data Center and dock with it. Some form of wireless communication protocols could also be part of the handshake along with these aerial movements, providing some kind of physical "identification signature". UFO movements have also been observed to be accompanied by patterns of strong visible light of various colors emitted by these spacecrafts at various parts of their structure. The best kind of wireless communications could still be "jammed" or communications antennas and its surfaces could become inoperative during space travels. Thus, identification by aerial movements might be the most effective way to prove your legitimacy of presence rather than be blown out of the sky by the Alien Data Center trying to defend its facilities against the incoming potential malicious alien attack. A combination of aerial handshakes could also be used, in this case, the UFO will string together a series of standard movements into a new pattern, a kind "access key" or a kind of encoded aerial pattern. Each of the patterns in Figure 21 could be a specific identification key, perhaps keys to indicate the type of its data payload or type of the Quantum Device it is transporting. The possibilities are endless where I think further research should be conducted into this area to learn more of.

There is also a possibility that the Alien Data Centre which the particular UFO was trying to interface with is a type of "Dark Data Center". As we know, a "Dark Data Center" is an unmanned data center where its management is fully automated or controlled by remotely and not staffed by personnel, in this case by Alien engineers.

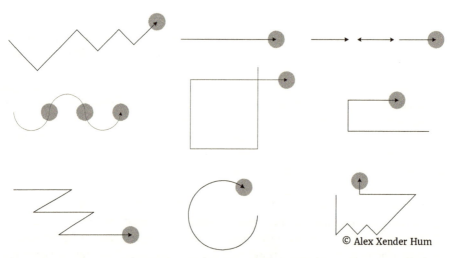

© Alex Xender Hum

Figure 21: Movements and maneuvers of UFOs – Unpredictable, irregular, zig-zags, sharp bends, wild accelerations, instant decelerations, sudden stops. Moving at high speeds, at any altitudes, arriving from nowhere and departing without a trace. (Alex X. Hum)

Some of the most common UFO shapes, those that are highly repeated in reported observations, are listed in Table 1. A large number of UFOs were sighted with the presence of bright sharp light emitting from various parts of the spacecraft, with most notably almost all instances either spotted at night or when the sun is near the horizon. Not all of the UFO effects reported by news stories can be explained by mirages or hot air balloons or some kind of weather apparatus. Commercial and Air

Force pilots have reported seeing unidentified objects accelerating at crazy speeds in different unpredictable directions (nothing resembling a normal fight plan), often at right angles or sinusoidal or flying away at impossible high-speeds as quickly as they arrived onto the scene.

There have also been many sightings of two or more UFOs uniting or assembling to form a larger object before finally flying off. I can imagine that these UFOs could be returning to other destinations each transporting different precious data or even objects - UFO data couriers of some kind.

Table 1: 12 UFO Shapes – Most common types of UFO shapes ("forms") and frequency of sightings. "Dome Saucer Type I" is the most common of all. Illumination marks ⁜ and ▊▊▊▊ indicate glows and positions of sharp light source, respectively. "Function" of each UFO type indicates its purpose and quantum function. (Alex X. Hum)

UFO Type	UFO Shape (Form)	Quantum Function
Saucer Type I (most common) - Circular shape from the top and during steep banking maneuvers	Dome Saucer	Quantum Information Transporter (Type 1) – Large data set - Quantum Crystal Beams
Saucer Type II	Lenticular Saucer or Disk with complete dome	Quantum Information Transporter (Type 2) – Middle data set – Quantum Crystal Beams
Saucer Type III	Lenticular with Dome	Quantum Information Transporter (Type 3) – Small data set – Quantum Crystal Beams
Top Hat		Quantum Servers (Type 1) – Large
Double Hat		Quantum Servers (Type 2) - Larger

Sphere		Quantum Crystals (Type 1) - Quantum Network equipment - Quantum Crystal Beams (Larger)
Conical Hat or Bell		Quantum Crystals (Type 2) - Quantum Network Equipment - Quantum Crystal Beams (Large)
Saturn		Quantum Power Source - Time Crystal Beams
Ellipsoidal (Egg)	 Hovering During Flight	Quantum Memory - Quantum Entangled storage media
Cylindrical (least common)		Alien Personnel Transporter (Type 1)
Dirigible, Airship or Oval (least common)		Alien Personnel Transporter (Type 2) - Large
Triangle or Boomerang (A)	 Delta Equilateral A	Alien Reconnaissance Vehicle - Alien Data Center Defenders

As we have seen in the Sections on "Quantum Entanglement for Teleportation" and "Teleporting Quantum Information" on pages 45 and 47 respectively, we would need two or more sets of Quantum Entangled Crystal devices in order to teleport information instantaneously across the vast expanse of space, i.e. from one alien location to the Alien Data Center on Earth. Once the sets of Quantum-entangled crystals have been created at a data center base, the UFOs will transport them to the designated location of the Alien Data Center for integration into the Alien data network. The dimensions or sizes of the UFO are related to the amount of data it is designed to transport and also dependent on the type of its mission.

Once fully installed, the quantum-entangled UFO and with its crystal payload will start to receive quantumly-teleported data and information instantaneously from the originating transmitting data centers, thanks to the power of quantum entanglement. The roles could also be reversed, whereby any information or data collected and processed at the Earth-based Alien Data Center will instantaneously be quantum-teleported without any loss of time to any locations connected to it. Another one of data center architecture principles is 'Scalability and Resiliency'. We can imagine the networks of Alien Data Centers installed on Earth is replicated across the universe within every crystal-based planet and star. With such an interconnected Alien data network, all knowledge and wisdom are shared to create and maintain an universal consciousness engine that can somehow influence world events and perhaps nurture and guide the intellectual advancements or evolutions of the local inhabitants - a theory I have proposed in Sections "I think, therefore I am" and "Infinitely ever-expanding Data and Information" on pages 14 and 16 respectively.

A truly remarkable alien master architecture of intergalactic data-sharing network infrastructure to exert their influence of collective existence onto the local inhabitants!

△ △ △

Alien Teachers and Messengers

There have been many sightings of UFOs flying in and out of our oceans, in the lakes, harbors and lagoons. This may suggest these Unidentified Submerged Objects (USOs) are entering or exiting their underwater bases which they operate out from. The term "USO" was born when alleged sightings of extraterrestrial spacecraft emerging from under the water surface began to gain in prominence and public awareness of this kind of new phenomenon. Analyzing these sightings reveal the underwater bases tend to concentrate in the coasts off of Southern California, Puerto Rico and other locations. The US Navy submarine division has been recording and logging ultra fast-moving underwater objects in excess of 200 knots (normally submarines and torpedoes can only move up to a maximum of 40 knots).

While locations of UFO sightings have been recorded all over the planet, there is none more amazing than to 'catch' UFOs emerging out of mountains, volcanoes and splashing out of water surfaces. The reverse is also true of UFOs shooting into bodies of water and becoming USOs adding an extra dimension of mystery, curiosity and wonder.

The locations of Alien bases have been very difficult to pinpoint. My theory is that they are difficult to locate because these bases are places where giant crystal caves are! We have learned that giant crystal caves have been discovered hundreds of meters deep underground and in places that are hard for humans to access. To get to these crystal caves, one would need special entrances or openings of some kind that would be concealable from unauthorized access. One design principle of data centers is 'Security Access Control'. I would imagine that Alien Architects would be protecting the concealed access points and base entrances as much as we would be doing the same today with our secret bases, military and otherwise.

I believe that one of the many underwater and submerged Alien Data Centers could be in the still dark waters of Lake Titicaca on the borders of Peru and Bolivia (Figure 22). Lake Titicaca is not only the world's highest body of navigable waters and host to a plethora of UFO and USO activities but also located at the "Ring of Fire". Is the latter observation a coincidence? There have been numerous reports of UFOs entering into the lake, remaining submerged as USOs potentially docking with the Alien Data Center hidden there, and later on, shooting out of the lake and disappearing into the sky as UFOs. The transition between UFOs and USOs was truly amazing and has led many to believe this is some kind of advanced and possible Ancient Alien base there. We know of course the base is some kind of alien data center.

Figure 22: Map of Lake Titicaca − The Tiwanaku historical site is about 20km south-east of the lake. Pumapunku is about 1km south-west of this Tiwanaku historical site.

The ancient city of Tiwanaku, sitting on the south-eastern shore of Lake Titicaca, is considered to be one of the world's oldest cities in the world. The advanced levels of enlightenment in advanced agriculture, irrigation, astronomy, buildings and structures that suggest advanced applications of engineering and machinations have led many ancient astronaut theorists and ufologists to suggest that an extraterrestrial race once resided there. With an array of numerous texts and statues found in the surroundings of Lake Titicaca, seemingly depicting some kind of ancient

Mesopotamian underwater gods, these researchers suggested that the artefacts were from an alien civilization that once resided beneath the calm unsuspecting blue waters of Lake Titicaca. In 2013, a group of explorers was drawn to the lake by a large circular submerged object slowly moving across the lake away from the shoreline. The USO maintained its shape during its movement suggesting it is solid in construction. Could it be one of the UFO Saucer of Type I lurking in the lake?

The part that gets me into thinking a bit deeper is that, at regions of sightings at UFO-to-USO-to-UFO transitions, the local residents in those areas had enjoyed increased and heightened levels of thinking, science, engineering and intellect in that they usually produced unbelievable out-of-this-world architectures, buildings, time-keeping and time-predicting machines and walls and walls of giant perfectly-angled marble blocks, probably by the use of advanced engineering capabilities. This happened at Tiwanaku, Bolivia. How did the ancient people of Tiwanaku come to possess knowledge of advanced engineering and machinations, agriculture and irrigation techniques? Could this be related to the alien phenomenon observed there?

Tiwanaku is a UNESCO World Heritage Site, administered by the Bolivian government. Also known as Tiahuanaco, Tiwanaku is an archeological site in western Bolivia near Lake Titicaca and it is one of the largest such sites in South America. The surface area of Tiwanaku covers around 4 square kilometers and is organized over the area of decorated ceramic structures, monuments and megalithic blocks of perfectly cut dimensions. The site is believed to be at least 10,000 years old. The exciting phenomenon of Tiwanaku is its structures - which include the Akapana, Kalasasaya and Puma-Punku (also known as Pumapunku). Tiwanaku is very significant in Inca traditions because it is believed to be the place where the world was created.

Pumapunku is part of a large temple complex of Tiwanaku. Pumapunku is a terraced kind of earthen mound of 167.36m (549.1 feet) wide along its north-south axis and 116.7m (383 feet) wide along its east-west axis. See Figure 23.

Figure 23: Pumapunku – Fortified with layers of tall precision-fitted stone walls (top right, bottom right). Full of engineering marvels and evidence of the use of advanced machinations and tools at Tiwanaku.

What is so amazing to me about Pumapunku is that is laced with strange looking red stone blocks of pure precision engineering techniques. The terrace is paved with multiple enormous stone blocks of which the largest stone block measures 7.81m (25.6 feet) tall by 5.17m (17.0 feet) wide by 1.07m (3.5 feet) deep. Based on the specific gravity of the red sandstone from which it was carved from, this monolithic block is estimated to weigh 131 tons (131,000 kilograms). The second largest stone block is 7.90m (25.0 feet) tall by 2.50m (8 feet 2 inch) wide by 1.86m (6 feet 1 inch) deep and weighs about 85.21 tons (85,210 kilograms). Both of these stone blocks are standing in a part of the so-called *Plataforma Litica* – a large stone terrace of 6.75m (22.5 feet) × 38.72m (129 feet) in dimension- and composed of red sandstone believed to be transported up a steep incline from a quarry near Lake Titicaca roughly 10 to 100km (6.2 to 62 miles) away.

In assembling the walls of the Pumapunku fortress, each stone was finely 'cut' and accurately interlocked with its surrounding blocks that fit together like a puzzle- this is evident in Figure 24 – forming load-bearing joints without the use of mortar. The precision of the 'stone-cutting' engineering challenges today's engineering methods. The level of precision is mind-boggling. A trademark of Pumapunku is perhaps the "H" blocks, one of the best examples of lost ancient technology and machinations. The perfection of lines and contours consistently presented on each "H" block presents staggering feats of cutting perfect right-angle edges around and within each block at narrow proximity to each step and corners. It is not only the perfectly-level and straight cuttings but also the consistent shaping that is so amazing – almost like all the blocks were manufactured by a mega-factory with assembly lines. Another great feat of Pumapunku's ancient engineering is a series of small holes (diameter of 4mm or about 5/32th inch) perfectly 'drilled' into hard rock at exact equal distances of 32.5mm (about 1 9/32th inch) apart from top to bottom and with no chipped edges. These blocks are sculpted out of very hard Andesite rock whose Mohs Hardness Index is more than 7.5 (Mohs index of diamond is at 10). It can be imagined that this fantastic stonework was created with some highly advanced tools and machines, because it was proven that modern tools today were not able to reproduce such exquisite work with the exact precisions and tolerances and importantly, with factory-like consistency. It is interesting to know that Andesite is formed at convergent plate boundaries caused by tectonic movements, which is where "Ring of Fire" is and which also includes the west coast of South America, exactly where Pumapunku and Tiwanaku are located.

Figure 24: Giant Monolithic Stone Blocks – Perfectly-cut and meticulously shaped "H" blocks stacked neatly into walls (bottom left, bottom right). Stone blocks with highly-polished faces (top left, top right). Evidence of small holes drilled at equidistant space apart at very high precision into solid hard rock (top left, center, center right).

There is a grand sense of elegance and beauty and yet a mysterious and awesome feeling of power and wisdom when appreciating these out-of-this-world engineering achievements of wonder at Pumapunku.

How did the people of Pumapunku manage to produce such works of perfection, elegance and precision? How did these people manage to cut, transport and even stack these huge mega-ton stone blocks to tight perfections without the use of some kind of 'alien' technology? I think I have a theory to explain this.

I believe this has everything to do with the UFO activities around Lake Titicaca and Tiwanaku. The visitations of UFOs to this area, as I suggested, is due to the presence of the Alien Data Center bases in the area. The knowledge stored in the highly advanced forms of crystal devices, transported by the 'Lake Titicaca UFOs' and which were then integrated into the alien bases, 'revealed' themselves as "Messengers" to the ancient Tiwanaku people in the area. I believe there was some kind of knowledge transfer of alien technologies of precision sculpting of stone structures and transportation of heavy objects to the ancient native people. These alien technologies are actually applications of crystal devices which I have discussed in Chapter "Incredible Powers of Crystals" on page 43. I believe the people of Pumapunku were 'gifted' with advanced alien knowledge of building and operating high-powered lasers – for high-precision cutting and sculpting stone blocks; and the knowledge and application of using Quantum Time-Crystals for phasing stone blocks into light-weight materials, easily transporting and assembling them into densely packed patterns and then rephrasing them back into proper stone blocks once set into place.

I believe there are Alien Data Centers which actually might be secretly staffed with highly-skilled Alien Engineers tasked with managing the operations of the facilities. UFOs of Cylindrical and Dirigible types could be the transporter of choice due to its larger size and volume. I think there could be possibilities that there was some kind of interactions between these curious Alien Engineers (after all, engineers are creators and builders, even Alien ones I suppose) and the ancient Pumapunku people. These Aliens could be the "Alien Teachers" imparting their creation knowledge and wisdom.

Two very interesting structures at Tiwanaku are the "Gate of the Sun" with its "Calendar Wall", as shown in Figure 25. The "Gate of the Sun" has the Inca Sun god "Viracocha" ingrained at its top center. The "Calendar Wall" was discovered to be a Sun and Moon calendar calculator. When an observer stands at the "Observation Stone" at a distance of 58m facing the center of the "Calendar Wall", which is the west wall of Kalasasaya (the courtyard), and by marking the positions of the Sun setting at one of the eleven stone pillars on the "Calendar Wall", the observer can 'see' the respective times of the Winter Solstice sunset (21 June), Summer Solstice sunset (21 December), the Autumn Equinox sunset (22 March, indicating the beginning of Autumn) and the Spring Equinox (22 September, indicating the beginning of Spring). Figure 25 shows the top view of Kalasasaya with the geometry of where the "Observation Point" is in relation to the "Calendar Wall". How the Solar calendar calculator works is illustrated in Figure 27. Essentially it is a very clever technique for the observer to quickly tell the time of the year at precisely that moment in time, and instantly know the number of days to certain significant dates of celebrations or ancient holidays in the future or the past.

As Tiwanaku is the Southern Hemisphere, it must be remembered that *winter* in Tiwanaku is *summer* in the Northern hemisphere. This means that 21 June is Tiwanaku's Winter Solstice and it is also Stonehenge's Summer Solstice. Not only a Solar calendar, the "Calendar Wall" is also a sophisticated Lunar calendar based on

88

sidereal lunar months. Instructions on how to use the Solar and Lunar Calendar were carved into the rock face of the "Gate of the Sun".

Could these constructions be a way to prepare for the coming of the "Alien Teacher" or something else?

Figure 25: Wonders of Tiwanaku - "Gate of the Sun"(right) and the "Calendar Wall" to the left of it.

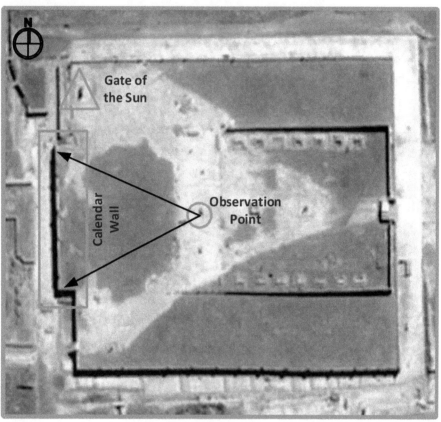

Figure 26: Top view of Kalasasaya (courtyard of Tiwanaku) – Position of the "Observation Point" at 58m (193 feet 4 inch) from the center of the "Calendar Wall". "The Gate of the Sun" is at the top left. (Alex X. Hum)

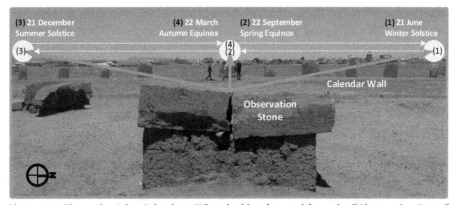

Figure 27: Tiwanaku Solar Calendar - When looking forward from the "Observation Stone" towards the "Calendar Wall" as shown, the position of the Sun setting charts the movement of the Sun in the Southern hemisphere where Tiwanaku is. Over the course of the year, the positions of the sunsets move to the left over each pillar on the "Calendar wall", from position (1) to (2) to (3) and then moving right to position (4) and finally back to position (1). Each numbered position indicates the beginning of the respective Solstices for the people of Tiwanaku and possibly the entire continent. (Alex X. Hum)

The phenomenon of plotting and calculating the positions of the sunsets with pillars on calendar walls or monuments by local natives is truly amazing. In fact, this phenomenon is not unique to Tiwanaku but has been discovered at many other locations around the world.

This 'sun-watching' phenomenon is affectionately known as the "Sun Cult" or "Sun Worshipping". In fact, the oldest solar observatory in the Americas has been found, pointing to the existence of "Sun Cults" thousands of years into our ancient past.

The structure found in the Chankillo archeological site in Peru, comprises a group of thirteen 2,300-year-old towers known as the "Thirteen Towers". The towers helped chart the annual rising and setting positions of the Sun across the sky, providing a natural solar calendar or solar calculator to mark special dates for the ancient natives (Towers Point to Ancient Sun Cult, 2007). Each tower structure of "Thirteen Towers" has a pair of staircases built inside them leading to the top, presumably to serve as observation towers or perhaps as defensive positions. These structures are rectangular in shape (75 to 125m^2 or 807 to 1,345 square feet), 2-6m (6.67 to 20 feet) tall and are regularly spaced, from 4.7 to 5.1m (15 feet 8 inch to 17 feet), along the ridge of a low hill running from north to south, forming a magnificent 'saw-tooth' silhouette of a jaw line or the spiny back of a prehistoric dinosaur with narrow gaps at regular intervals. Figure 28 provides a perspective of the huge structures in Chankillo. So, from where do you observe the perspective of the arcs of traced by the Sun rising and setting thus in a way 'touching' the "Thirteen Towers". About 230m (750 feet) perpendicularly to the east and west of ridge, scientists believed there are two observation points (like the observation point in front of the "Calendar Wall" at Tiwanaku). From one of these two vantage points, the 300m (1000 feet) wide span of the towers (Tower 1 to Tower 13) from end to end along the horizon corresponds very closely to the rising and setting positions of the Sun over the calendar year.

If you were to stand at the western observation point, you would see the Sun coming up in the morning, and where it would appear at sunset at which one of the thirteen towers would depend on the time of year and thus this method would tell you what time of the year it is. Really cool! Let's take a closer look.

On Winter Solstice day, which is 21 June in Peru, if viewed from the western observation point, the Sun would *rise* slightly to the left of left-most tower i.e. Tower 1 (position (1) in Figure 28). This Winter Solstice Sun will then *set* directly at the right-most tower (Tower 1) when viewed from the eastern observation point (not in the figure). Over the course of the year from June to December, the Sun will rise at points gradually towards the right side along the ridge, finally approaching position (2) at Spring Equinox on 22 September. The towers along the sunset's approach from position (1) to position (2) will tell the other times of the year. At Summer Solstice on 21 December, the Sun will rise at position (3) directly above Tower 13, the right-most tower. From the Summer Solstice day onwards, the points of the Sunrise will now reverse along the path towards the left and return to position (4) on Autumn Equinox on 22 March, and finally back to position (1) thus completing one full year of the calendar or a complete orbit of the Earth round the Sun. Due to the north-south orientations of the Tower ridge with respective to the east and west locations of the observation points, there is little angular movements of between where the sun rises and where it sets behind the mountain range on opposite sides of Tower ridge.

On Winter Solstice day, which is 21 June in Peru, if we now viewed the Towers from the eastern observation point, the Sun would set directly at the right-most tower i.e. Tower 1. Hence, the interpretation of the time of the year is dependent on which observation point you are observing from and also if you are observing for sun rises or sunsets.

Figure 28: "Thirteen Towers" at Chankillo (Chanquillo), Peru - With our reference at the Western Observation point, on Winter Solstice day on 21 June, the Sun rises slightly to the left of Tower 1 (position (1)). During the course of the year, the Sun will rise at points gradually towards the right above the towers toward position (2) on Spring Equinox on 22 September. The path of the sunrise traverses towards the right to position (3) directly above Tower 13 on Summer Solstice day on 21 December. From this point on, the sunrise will reverse direction towards the left, reaching position (4) on Autumn Equinox on 22 March. Finally, the sunrise will return to position (1) on Winter Solstice day on 21 June. (Alex X. Hum)

Similar sun-observation structures are found across the world such as in Cusco, Peru, Easter Island, and also Stonehenge, England. The presence and constructions of these structures to carefully map out the journey of the Sun across the sky and accurate measurements to calculate the time of the year really emphasize the passion of these ancient natives. Researchers believe these "Sun Cults" or "Sun Worshippers" are tribes of people who rely on these time-telling instruments for accurate timings of the year for irrigation and crop growing purposes. I have a different theory of something else.

I wrote earlier, in Section "UFOs: Information Transporters" on page 73, about the true purpose of UFOs - transporting data to the Alien Data Center hidden in underwater bases in Lake Titicaca. The shapes of these UFOs happened to be circular in form like saucers – the most common being the Dome-shaped Saucers of Type I. These flying saucer types are the Alien data transporters which deliver the precious crystal-based quantum devices (see types and functions of UFOs in Table 1). It must be really majestic if one was lucky to observe the movements (take a look at Figure 21) of the flying saucer rising into the sky and the moment it dives into the waters. When these crystalline flying saucers or flying discs make steep 90-degree banking maneuvers and barrel-rolls in flights, they surely will look like a full-circular disc, and not just any disc but a shining brightly lit disk, just like the Sun flying forwards to greet you! Must have been an awe-inspiring experience worth to share with future generations.

I believe the ancient people of Peru and Bolivia were actually worshipping these Sun-lit flying saucers and built amazing solar-calendar monuments to honor and celebrate the arrivals and departures of their Alien Teachers and Messengers to mimic the 'supernatural' way how they swopped down into the horizon like a perfect 10 Olympic diver and how they would shoot up out of the waters into skies; maneuvers such as these would be characteristic of the superior maneuverability prowess afforded by their spacecrafts. Sights of 'reflective' sun-lit and glowing 'moon-lit' UFOs entering and exiting the waters or behind mountains had deeply inspired and motivated the natives into engineering and building intricate, complex and advanced instruments such as these Solar and Lunar Calendars to forever remember and commemorate their out-of-the-world encounters with their Alien Teachers Mentors. These UFOs could be trying to camouflage or disguise their approaches (discussed in Section "Invisibility" on page 71) but instead had unintended consequences of indirectly opened the minds of observers. Truly, UFO and Alien encounters had certainly 'mined' the best engineering and enlightenment of intellectual out of the observers.

The *General Theory of Aliens* (GTA) is sightings of UFOs and potential encounters with UFOs and Alien beings have inspired ancient civilizations for thousands of years. UFOs possess superior technologies that have prevented digital detections and have cleverly utilized special properties of crystals to remain undetectable and invisible. Motivated to impress their other worldly "Alien Teachers" and to encourage contact and thus to communicate with their revered teachers, ancient civilizations built beautiful and worthy monuments shaped like giant forms of crystals and function like solar calendars, and often encoded with universal mathematical formulas and constants in their architecture forms. To center their worship and philosophy, ancient people cleverly encoded the circular disk shapes of their flying objects to resemble the Sun and Moon into their line of design of advanced solstice calculations and built mighty stone structures to express them. The **GTA** is the spacecrafts of the Aliens come in various forms – the most common shape is the dome-shape saucer and is the most often and regularly sighted object – with various functions as cosmic transporters of quantum crystal data and other quantum computing devices to build, maintain and operate their base of Alien Data Centers. Ancient natives have shown their skills and will to build physical forms of structures to make contact with their revered "Alien Teachers" who had taught their advanced science of engineering, machinations and tools, agriculture, irrigation and more.

In Section "Ring of Fire" on page 114, I will explain why it is not surprising to know that these UFO and USO sightings tend to be located at or near the "Ring of Fire". In a similar line of thought, centers of advanced ancient civilizations tend to sprout up and concentrate near the "Ring of Fire".

"'CAUSE AND EFFECT is the wheel of life. A broken shaft ruins the ride. Walk the Enlightened path, feel the light.' - wisdom gifted by Peng*Xen."

7

Alien Protocol
◎ Contact and Communication ◎

✳

"THE DISK reappeared at Axiom:Heart instantly, performing a signature high-speed aerial maneuver with a subtle yet intense lightshow. Permission granted to dock."

Communicating with Aliens have been attempted by Earthlings but we have yet to receive any response. Perhaps Aliens had communicated back but we just didn't know how to interpret and respond back to their first messages and thus things stopped in translation.

In the world of telecommunications, a meaningful communication protocol is required, which comprises a standard of rules that allows more than two entities of a communications network to transmit and receive information. Communications is a very basic form of contact with new communities and even alien beings. The protocol defines the strength, range, rules and syntax, data formats, semantics, data structure, security and identification, and timing synchronizations of communication channels, and error-recovery algorithms. The transmitting party almost always are required to identify itself before it is authorized to complete the communication channel with the receivers. Protocols can be implemented by hardware, software or a hybrid combination of both. In other words, communication protocols can be implemented by physical or non-physical means or a hybrid blend of both. Simplistically, we just need to agree on the communication protocol and format so to be able to understand the messages we exchanged with each other so to conduct meaningful conversations.

The important thing about meaningful information exchange is that all communicating parties need to agree the set of well-defined data formats to be able to exchange meaningful messages amongst them. Each message has an exact meaning embedded with the purpose to elicit a response from a range of possible responses which would have been pre-determined. The specified behavior is independent of how the protocol is implemented. Protocols could include mutually-agreed methods to prevent unauthorized parties from listening in and intercepting their communications.

Ancient civilizations had been intrigued with the 'supernatural' powers of crystals, crystal forms and obelisks – also refer to Chapter "Incredible Powers of Crystals" on page 43 - and had tirelessly manifested and transformed their fascinations into various physical forms of pyramid-like shapes and advanced "UFO"-observation instruments like Solar calendars we discussed previously. I believe these structures are the very first physical symbols of the communication protocol which ancient civilizations used to connect with their "Alien Teachers".

If we were the ancient natives who had been deeply inspired, now exceptionally motivated and emotionally moved to make the first contact and then to communicate with the Alien beings flying in their 'supernatural' flying objects visiting the local areas, how and where would you start to 'catch' their attention or even to show your worthiness for their attention?

As the first and foremost basic step, it has to start with some kind of physical forms of a communication or contact protocol to initiate your contact with the other party. Perhaps a meaningful gift of some kind.

The structure of the physical 'protocol format' would need to be permanent, meaningful, striking, attractive. And, for a higher chance of encounter, the physical protocol format must express some level of high intelligence, perhaps encode some demonstrations of previous teachings or mementos into their architectures, built into it to get the attention of Aliens who have been doing their very best to avoid detection and possibly to ignore you.

Where would the ancient natives get their ideas and examples of structures to build a model of this physical protocol?

I believe the ancient natives most likely acquired their ideas of giant crystal beams when they caught glimpses of such objects while Alien Engineers were off-loading them into their bases for integration with their data centers. Ancient people have always been fascinated by giant crystal beams leading many ancient civilizations to build giant obelisks and pyramids as monuments or even worshipping them - refer to Chapter "Fascinated by Giant Crystals" on page 31.

Mesoamerican pyramids or pyramid-shaped structures have formed a prominent feature of the ancient Mesoamerican architectural landscape and has become magnificent awe-inspiring landmarks. Ancient Egyptian pyramids had set the benchmarks for Obelisk and Crystal Beam design and construction. These Mesoamerican pyramids looked familiar and also adopted more interactive human-centric designs and intricate details setting them apart on a new branch of pyramidal obelisk architecture.

The Mesoamerican instances most usually include terraces, steps and ramp structures with temples on the top terrace, somewhat has some resemblance with the ziggurats of Mesopotamia rather than the pyramids of Ancient Egypt. This differentiation in design and usage (spanning across 1 to 2 thousand years) is expected because interpretations of Alien encounters and understanding will be different leading to slightly differentiated designs. The important thing to note is that all these designs can be classified as belonging to the family of Pyramidions and Pyramids.

Many Mesoamerican civilizations, dynasties and cultures made up the rich historical landscapes of the region spanning at least five thousand years ago. The cultures that have gifted us, by way of archeologists having discovered their pyramid-like structures, include Aztec, Maya, Teotihuacan, Toltec, classical Veracruz, and Zapotec. Of these cultures, the Maya left the largest number of pyramid-like monuments.

The Maya are a people of southern Mexico and northern Central America with at least 3,000 years of history and artefacts. Archeological evidence shows the Maya started to build ceremonial architectures about 3,000 years ago, marking it next to the ancient age of Ancient Egypt. The earliest monuments include stair-stepped pointed pyramids with many of each fitted with a top terrace or platform upon which a smaller ceremonial room was constructed, probably dedicated as a place of Sun worship.

Of the thousands of pyramids the Maya built, there are more than 30 that are very well-defined and preserved structures. One of them is the "El Castillo" Pyramid (see Figure 29) at Chichen-Itza. Chichen-Itza is a large city built by the Maya people of the Terminal Classic period, in the eastern part of Yucatan Peninsula in Mexico. The archeological site is located in the Tinúm Municipality there. A UNESCO World Heritage site, "El Castillo" is also known as the "Temple of Kukulkan" which is a Mesoamerican step pyramid that dominates the center of the Chichen-Itza archeological site. The limestone structure is more formally designated by archeologists as Chichen Itza Structure 5B18 and was constructed by the pre-Columbian Maya civilization sometime between 8th and 12th BCE. El Castillo served as the temple to the god Kukulkan, the Yucatec Maya's "Feathered Serpent" deity. The pyramid consists of a series of square flat terraces with steep stairways ascending up each face of the pyramid to the top where there is a room.

"El Castillo", shown in Figure 29, has quite a few amazing secrets. Sculptures of two plumed serpents each winding down the two sides of the north-facing balustrade. At the spring and autumn equinoxes of the year, the late afternoon sun strikes off the northwest corner of the pyramid and casts a series of triangular shadows against the northwest balustrade, creating a magical animation-like illusion of the feathered serpent "Kukulkan" 'slithering' its way down each side of the temple pyramid. The second of El Castillo's secrets is each of the pyramid's four sides has 91 steps which, when added all sides together and adding the temple platform at the very top as the 'final' step, produces a total of 365 steps, equal to the number of days of the Maya year. The entire structure is 30m (100 feet) tall including the 6m (20 feet) height of the temple.

Stepping back for about 200m (666 feet 8 inch) from the base of the pyramid and looking up, it is quite easy to recognize the "El Castillo" pyramid resembles the tip of a crystal beam; it would look similar to the top half of a 'single-termination point' Obelisk. Imagine if we were to flatten the steps, smooth out terraces and sharpened the top platform of "El Castillo", it will look exactly like the tip of a Giant Obelisk.

I consider "El Castillo" to be one of the most special structures dedicated as faith to the "Alien Teacher" because it encompasses two significant "Alien Worship" artefacts – the first one is the crystal obelisk structure representing the giant Alien crystal beams found in Alien Data Centers, and the second is the built-in Sun-observation instrument - to honor the Alien sun-lit flying saucers. Building meaningful knowledge – of astronomical science and mathematics - into their monuments is a kind of encoding protocol in their messages, which the natives used to stimulate contact with their "Alien Teachers".

Figure 29: "El Castillo" Pyramid at Chichen-Itza – 'Single-termination point' Giant Crystal Beam pointing skywards into the heavens. (S. Hamsilo)

Figure 30: "Kukulkan" at Chichen-Itza – North-face of the pyramid (left) with the two feathered serpents "Kukulkan" guarding the bottom of the stairs. At the Spring and Winter Solstices, Kukulkan will 'slither' animatedly down the steps (right).

Unlike Chichen-Itza's "El Castillo" pyramid and many pyramids, one pyramid at Coba, Mexico, allows the enthusiastic explorer to climb its ancient steps right up to its top. The "Nohoch Mul-Ixmoja" Pyramid is 42m (140 feet) tall and 130 steps to the top. It is the second tallest Maya structure on the Yucatán Peninsula, exceeded by Pyramid "Calakmul" at 45 meters (150 feet). The first step of wide stairs rises up from the ground, ever increasing at a perfect precise incline. Climbing the smoothened stone steps and looking up, the pyramid has transformed into a giant 'single-termination point' crystal beam pointing proudly into the heavens.

The Coba site is the nexus of the largest network of stone causeways or paths of the ancient Maya civilization, with many intricately engraved and sculpted stelae that documented ceremonial life stories and important events. Sacbeob or sacbes are raised stone pathways that connected clusters of residential areas to the main center of Coba and the all-important water sources, potentially linking the cenotes (natural underground reservoirs of water) in the limestone region. Thanks to tracing the networks of Sacbeob paths, maps leading to the discovery of Coba and other ancient sites became possible.

With temperatures of 27 to 32°C (81 to 90F) high throughout the year, pyramid building in the lush green vegetation can take on a breath-taking meaning to the ancient builders.

Figure 31: Pyramid "Nohoch Mul-Ixmoja" at Coba, Mexico – A remarkable view awaits the avid explorer at the top. 42m (140 feet) tall and 130 steps. (Choying Lhamo)

Uxmal, which means "Thrice built or occupied" or the "Place of Abundant Harvests", is an ancient Maya city of the classical period in Yucatan, Mexico. Together with Chichen-Itza in Mexico and Tikal in Guatemala, Uxmal is considered as one of the most important archeological sites of Maya culture. Uxmal has been designated a UNESCO World Heritage site in recognition of its significance to culture, history and science. In Uxmal, there is a uniquely shaped pyramid. "Adivino", also known as the "Pyramid of the Magician" is a smooth-face stepped pyramidal structure. This structure is unusual among other Maya structures because its cross-section is oval or elliptical in shape instead of the more common rectilinear cross-section. As a common practice of other Maya pyramids, where new temple pyramids were built on top of older ones, the "Adivino" newer pyramidal component was built as centered slightly to the east of the older smaller pyramid so that on the west side, the temple on top of the older pyramid is preserved with the newer temple above it, next to other even older temples. Another interesting feature of "Adivino" is its western staircases, they are situated to face the setting sun on the summer solstice day.

The Uxmal pyramid resembles a 'multi-terminal point' crystal beam with a smooth elliptical-shaped outer body. This structure like "El Castillo" has similar "Alien Teacher" features as symbolisms.

Figure 32: "Adivino" – Also known as the "Pyramid of the Magician" in Uxmal, Mexico. A smooth-face stepped pyramid of the Maya period.

Tikal is the ruin of an ancient city in northern Guatemala. A UNESCO World Heritage Site, in Tikal there is a series of "arrow-head" pyramids. Its first pyramid is the "Tikal Temple I", also known as the Temple of the Jaguar, with a height of 47m (154 feet). In Tikal, there is also another "arrow-head" pyramid called the "Tikal Temple II", also known as the Temple of the Masks, it stands at a total height of 42m (138 feet) and is situated opposite "Tikal Temple I". Spanning across Mesoamerica lies hundreds if not thousands of pyramidal structures. For some of the most wonderful mega structures, we have to look to the Aztec civilization.

Figure 33: "Arrow-head" Pyramids of Tikal - "Tikal Temple I" (left); "Tikal Temple II" (right).

From the Aztecs, the city of Teotihuacan is an ancient Mesoamerican city located in the State of Mexico 40 kilometers (25 miles) northeast of modern-day Mexico City. The Náhuatl name of Teotihuacan means the "City of the Gods" or "the place where the gods are created". Teotihuacan, a UNESCO World Heritage Site, is known today as the site of many of the most architecturally significant Mesoamerican pyramids. At its height, perhaps in the first half of the 1st millennium CE, Teotihuacan had a population of 125,000 or more people, making it the largest city in the pre-Columbian Americas and today it is the most visited archeological site in Mexico with more than 4.1 million visitors in 2017. Teotihuacan is the home of the "multi-level" pyramids.

"Pyramid of the Sun" at Teotihuacan affords a very good example of the "Alien Teacher" style of worship monuments. It holds some amazing secrets of its own. The name "Pyramid of the Sun" comes from the Aztecs who visited the city of Teotihuacan hundreds of years after it was abandoned. No one yet knows the original name of the pyramid given to it by the natives of Teotihuacan. Two construction phases started around 100 CE, with its completed size of 223.48m (733.2 feet) across and 71.17m (233.5 feet) high, and also included the construction of an altar, atop of this "five tiered" pyramid, which did not survive but was replaced by the nearby "Temple of the Feathered Serpent".

"Pyramid of the Sun" is the third tallest pyramid in the world, just over half of the height of the Great Pyramid of Giza. Scientists believed there is mathematics encoded in its form. The dimensions of the pyramid had excited scientists who believed the Aztecs at Teotihuacan had secretly encoded the universal mathematical constant "π" (Pi) into the 'astronomical' design of this pyramid.

The Teotihuacan "π" has a value of 3.140, this value is obtained by dividing the length of a side of the pyramid's base by its height i.e. 223.48 divided by 71.17 gives a value of 3.140, very close to the value of π (~3.14159)! π is an irrational number which repeats itself and it is impossible to express it in exact form of a common fraction nor its decimal representation as it never ends and never settles into a permanently repeating pattern, except by this clever mathematical encoding. An encoding I believe any "Alien Teacher" would be proud of its student. To add to its significance, π can only be exactly expressed as the ratio of the circumference of a circle to its diameter. What could be more circular than the shape of the Alien flying disk! One wonders at these similarities!

The "Pyramid of the Sun" was built on a carefully selected spot of land to align with the Cerro Gordo mountain to the north, where scientists believed some of its architectural designs were aligned to sunrises and sunsets on specific dates of the year. Coincidentally, the pyramid was built over a man-made tunnel that leads to a "cave" about six meters (20 feet) beneath the center of the structure. More recent excavations suggested the "cave" could have served as a royal tomb. I believe the purpose of this underground structure was built as a symbol of the "Alien Data Center" base and represented Teotihuacan's belief in their "Alien Teachers". I believe there is a more significant belief.

This kind of man-made tunnel architectures leading to underground royal burial chambers have similar significance, to those royal burial chambers discovered in Egypt, to the pharaohs and their gods. I shall discuss this interesting topic in the Section "Valley of the Kings" on page 117.

Figure 34: "Pyramid of the Sun" at Teotihuacan, Mexico. Built over a man-made tunnel leading to a "cave" about 6m (20 feet) beneath the center of the pyramid.

Figure 35: "Pyramid of the Moon" at Teotihuacan, Mexico – The view from the "Pyramid of the Sun". Underground man-made tunnels beneath the pyramid potentially leading to caves.

At the Teotihuacan site, there exists the second largest pyramid in Teotihuacan called the "Pyramid of the Moon" (see Figure 35). It stands at a height of 43m (143 feet 4 inch) tall and has multiple levels with smooth faces. Archeologists found tunnels beneath the pyramid revealing it was renovated at least six times and each time the size of the pyramid was enlarged in honor of the "Great Goddess of Teotihuacan". Perhaps the tunnels lead to a hidden "cave" as did for the case of the "Pyramid of the Sun" adding to further expressions of wanting to unite with their "Alien Teacher". The "Plaza of the Moon" at the front of the "Pyramid of the Moon" leads into the "Avenue of the Dead" with the "Pyramid of the Sun" a short distance on the left and other smaller ceremonial pyramids flanking both sides of the avenue. The "Temple of the Feathered Serpent" is situated at the far end of the "Avenue of the Dead" on the left.

Mathematical encodings have yet to be discovered from its dimensions but still it is a magnificent expression of the natives' fascinations with 'single-termination point' giant crystal beams and astronomical events like calculating the times and dates of solstices.

Figure 36: View of Teotihuacan along its axis – Pyramid of the Sun (middle left) and Pyramid of the Moon (bottom). The "Temple of the Feathered Serpent" (top left) at the end of the "Avenue of the Dead".

Stonehenge, a UNESCO World Heritage Site, is the most architecturally sophisticated pre-historic stone circle in the world (See Figure 37). Located in Wiltshire, England, 3km (2 miles) west of Amesbury. Stonehenge consists of a ring of standing giant stones, with each erected stone around 4m (13 feet) high, 2.1m (7 feet) wide and weighing around 25 tons (25,000kg). Archeologists estimated it was constructed from 3,000 to 2,000 BCE with the earliest monuments dating back to around 8,000 BCE.

Built through the ages from 3,100 to 1,600 BCE, the people who built Stonehenge left no written records. Many aspects of Stonehenge, such as how it was built and serving what purposes, still today remain as debates around possible scientific and archeological theories. The intriguing 'gift' of the site is the alignments of the stones to the sunset of the winter solstice and the opposing sunrise of the summer solstice – the great Trilithon, the enveloping horseshoe arrangement of the five central

Trilithons, the heel stone and the embanked avenue leading to the revered site itself. The site's associations with astronomical calculations and its precise astronomical significance to its people are a matter for deep debate and substantial speculation. The entrance to the Stonehenge site is at the north-eastern part, precisely matched in direction of the midsummer (commonly known as the summer solstice) sunrise and midwinter (winter solstice) sunset of the period.

If we look down from the top at the center of the Stonehenge site, as shown in Figure 38, what do we see? Doesn't Stonehenge look like the form of an Alien Flying Saucer? Does the form not look like that of Saucer Type I, the Dome Saucer? I definitely think so. Stonehenge's circular form with a central circular dome-like structure, forming two concentric circles, looks very similar to the Dome Saucer of Type I shown in Table 1 on page 79. I believe the ancient builders of Stonehenge designed this specific form to 'etch' into the memories of future generations their encounters with the same set of "Alien Teachers" as did the people of Tiwanaku, Chankillo, Chichen-Itza and Teotihuacan in their respective ancient pasts. It seems to be a running ongoing theme leading to their inspired stone creations.

These massive stone structures, be it in the form of giant pyramids or stone circles, I believe, are examples of the "Alien Protocol", invented by the faithful believers and time-honored beneficiaries of the "Alien Engineers".

Figure 37: Stonehenge – Ancient stone-circle 'Sun Calendar and Astronomical Calculator', located in Wiltshire, England, with beginnings from 8500-7000 BCE. Actual construction of the first monuments started around 3,500 BCE. Clearly, Stonehenge evolved in several construction phases ranging over at least 1,600 years.

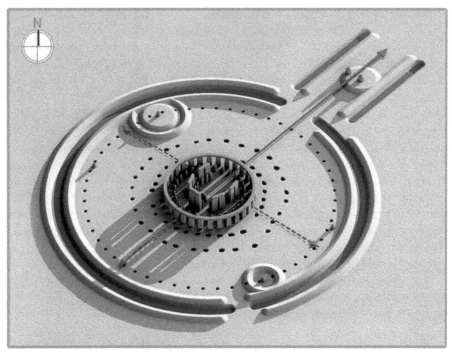

Figure 38: Complete Stonehenge – A computer rendered aerial view showing how the completed Stonehenge looks like a UFO of Flying Saucer Type I – Dome Saucer. The entrance to the site is at the north-east. A small exit can be seen at the south of the site.

As I discussed before, for any meaningful communication protocol to work would require a mutual set of handshakes between two communicating parties. With my belief that Stonehenge is an "Alien Teacher" monument, commemorating the arrivals and departures of Ancient Aliens to a "Crystal Cave" base nearby, where would the "protocol twin" of Stonehenge be? From NASA images of the Martian surface taken by space probes from the 1970s, researchers believed they have found Stonehenge's twin on Mars!

The stone circle on Mars, see Figure 39, was spotted on a raised burrow in images of the Martian surface captured by the HiRise camera on board the Mars Reconnaissance Orbiter. This "Stonehenge on Mars" is affectionately called "Marshenge". When we look at "Marshenge", it consists of two concentric circles at the outer rim, formed by some kind of a mound, and an inner circle of stone structures. The inner circle of larger stone structures closely resembles that of the 'blue' inner circle of Stonehenge. One interesting similarity between the two figures of Stonehenge and "Marshenge" is the presence of the horseshoe-shaped stone configuration at their centers, with the Stonehenge's version consisting of the giant Trilithon stones. The open end of the horseshoe of "Marshenge" points to the north-east, exactly similar to that of Stonehenge's. What a striking similarity of identity! I believe the purpose of "Marshenge" was like a kind of Solar Calendar to the native Martians as Stonehenge was a Solar Calendar and an "Alien Teacher" monument to the people of Stonehenge.

Could these two instances of stone-henges, one in England and the other on Mars, be the two physical communication formats of the "Alien Communication Protocol" theory? I do believe these two structures formed the agreed set of protocol signatures that could have enabled bilateral communications between the two Alien Data Center bases, one on Earth and the other on Mars. The two structures could also have been erected to honor their respective encounters with their "Alien Teachers" as did the people of ancient Tiwanaku and the Maya civilization. As Mars used to contain water coupled with its volcanic past, crystal caves would have definitely been by-products where Aliens could then grow their data centers within them, as how they did it on Earth.

Pyramidal structures have also been regularly spotted on Mars that have been linked to the ancient pyramids on Earth.

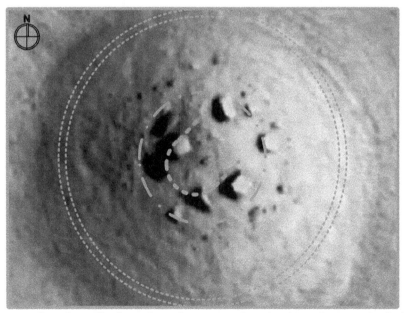

Figure 39: "Marshenge" – "Stonehenge"-on-Mars, the twin of Stonehenge on Earth. (Alex X. Hum)

The ***General Theory of Aliens*** (GTA) is ancient civilizations had been engaging in various monument-based forms of communications with their "Alien Teachers" and their UFOs. Ancient civilizations designed, built, and encoded messages of knowledge and wisdom into the structural designs of their pyramids, stone circles, solar calendar and calculators. Ancient civilizations designed monuments to reflect their appreciation and worship of alien artefacts, with their unique styles of architectures, to resemble Obelisks, circular and dome shapes of their 'supernatural' flying machines and to explicitly and artistically display their knowledge of astronomical mathematical constants or Golden ratios to impress their "Alien Teachers". Many magnificent representations of Alien-worship structures are found across today's South American countries in Peru, Bolivia and Mexico, and of course in Egypt, and other places across the world.

In the next chapter, I will introduce my theory on possible locations of the "Alien Data Centers", where their bases might be and how the ancient natives reacted to their presence.

"DISK'TA rolling sideways gliding effortlessly into dark blue waters. 'The waters swallowed up the Sun!', sings the welcoming natives prancing in circles punching the air."

8

Where are Alien Data Centers?

"JYU-N mindfully mended his way of life. Observing many sky-serpents twisting down the temple steps, Jyu-n whimpers seeing his fingers 'growing' back bit by bit, sometimes stopping sometimes starting. Deep gracious admiration for Peng*Xen floods his heart. All summer, the people far and wide celebrating their 'gifts', building beautiful mathematical monuments."

Alien data centers are mega structures of super advanced crystalline constructions called "Crystal Caves". Where would they be?

Well, we know that "Crystal Caves" are deep underground hermetically-sealed caverns of super crystal beams, manufactured out of a chemical mixture of heat, water and some kind of crystals. Where on Earth, it is actually in the earth, would one find such conditions? If we do a deep research of likeable locations for such crystal-making factories, I think we have to think big, really really big.

△ △ △

Ring of Fire

What is the "Ring of Fire"? The "Ring of Fire" (www.nationalgeographic.org) is a Pacific region home to a string of more than 500 volcanoes and sites of mega seismic activity, including three of the world's four most active volcanoes, around the edges of the Pacific Ocean. These 3 mega volcanoes are Mount St. Helens in the USA, Mount Fuji in Japan and Mount Pinatubo in the Philippines. It is also sometimes called the circum-Pacific Belt.

Most of 90% of the world's earthquakes and 80% of world's largest earthquakes take place along the "Ring of Fire", and the ring is dotted with 75% of all active volcanoes on Earth. What a very active intra-planetary-sized cauldron of tremendous fire, heat, pressure and water!

The "Ring of Fire" of today is not really shaped like a circular ring at all. It is shaped more like a 40,000 kilometer (25,000 mile) big horseshoe. See Figure 40. A string of almost regularly spaced 452 volcanoes stretches from the southern-tip of South America, winding up along west coast of North America, across the super long Bering Strait, down the length of Japan, and looping down to New Zealand. A few active and perhaps dormant volcanoes in Antarctica 'complete' up the Ring. As you can also see from Figure 40, the Ring is made up of multiple deep trenches of several kilometers deep around the 'perimeter' of the ring.

Figure 40: "Ring of Fire" – Earth's factories producing Giant Crystals Caves. Note that this is the shape and location of the "Ring of Fire" as of recent times. How would the "Ring of Fire" look like a 100 or 1,000 million years ago? Interestingly, Antarctica in the south is part of the Fire Ring.

The powerful movements of Tectonic plates – huge slabs of the Earth's crust fitting like pieces of a puzzle, created the "Ring of Fire". The plates are not fixed in place or time and are constantly moving on top of a layer of solid and molten rock called the mantle. These plates collide, move away from each other or slide next to each other.

At Plate Boundaries, three forms of boundary actions normally decide the consequences of these Tectonic movements – Convergent Actions, Divergent Actions and Transform Actions. One particular feature of the "Ring of Fire" where I am also particularly interested in is the "Hot-Spots".

"Hot Spots" are regions deep within the Earth's mantle from which extreme heat rises. The huge temperature difference facilitates the melting of earth rock in the brittle, upper portions of the mantle. Magma, which is melted rock, pushes through cracks in the crust to form volcanoes, be it on the surface of the earth or deep on the ocean floor.

As Magma courses through the earth's layers, it supplies constant streams of extreme heat to pockets of water that are hermetically sealed or trapped in huge caverns of underground crystal-making materials. This combination of the critical chemical ingredients resulted in the formation of "Mega Crystal Caves" very similar to the "Cave of Crystals" discovered in the Naica Mines in Mexico.

Popocatépetl is one of the most dangerous volcanic mountains in the "Ring of Fire". It is also one of Mexico's most active volcanoes, with more than 15 recorded eruptions since 1519. The volcano is situated on the Trans-Mexican Volcanic belt, as a result of the small Cocos Plate subducting beneath the North American Plate. While located close to urban regions of Mexico City and Puebla, Popocatépetl poses a risk to more than 20 million people living close by.

Is it a coincidence that the beautiful and wonderous "Cave of Crystals" is situated within the "Ring of Fire" and close to the volcano Popocatépetl? I don't think it is any coincidence at all. Alien Data Centers ARE "Mega Crystal Caves". We can infer that Alien Data Centers are highly located or, shall we say, most likely to be found in the "Ring of Fire" or near it.

It can be imagined that over millions of years of tectonic movements all over the planet even till today, there will be hundreds of millions of Crystal Caves everywhere in the Earth's Crust, in mountains or under the sea, not just in the "Ring of Fire" and regions around the area, each effectively functioning as Alien Data Centers with networks of super advanced crystal beams. Figure 40 shows how the "Ring of Fire" looks like in modern times with today's familiar positions of land masses and the boundaries of continents. Tectonic plate actions have always been in full force all over the planet since its birth about 4 billion years ago. What would the "Ring of Fire" look like 100 million years ago or even a billion years ago? Would the Ancient "Ring of Fire" be where today's Antarctica would be? Locations of Alien Data Centers back then would have been all over the world. The hypothesis that Alien Data Centers are located in the "Ring of Fire" may sound counter-intuitive but I assure you it is not. The hypothesis is actually true. Well, isn't there a favorite saying "The safest places to hide in are those places where people least expect to find you?"

△ △ △

Valley of the Kings

The Valley of the Kings, also known as the Valley of the Gates of the Kings, is a valley in Egypt where, for a period of nearly 500 years from the 16th to the 11th BCE, many tombs cut out from rocks were excavated to entomb pharaohs and powerful nobles as eternal resting places of the New Kingdom (the Eighteenth to the Twentieth Dynasties of Ancient Egypt). See Figure 41.

The valley is located at the west bank of the River Nile, opposite the ancient city of Thebes (modern Luxor), and within the heart of the Theban Necropolis (west bank of the River Nile). The site consists of two valleys, the East Valley (where the majority of the royal tombs are located) and the West Valley. Royal tombs were decorated with scenes from Egyptian mythology and contain clues and beliefs of the period, giving an idea of the opulence and power of the pharaohs.

The Valley of the Kings, home to over 60 tombs and burial chambers – ranging in sizes from KV54, a simple pit, to KV5, a complex tomb with over 120 chambers belong to the sons of Ramesses II, is 400 miles south of the Great Pyramids of Giza in Egypt. This area has been the focus of many archaeological and Egyptological explorations since the end of eighteenth century, and its tombs and burial chambers continue to stimulate theories, research and interest from the scholastic communities. In 1979, it became a UNESCO World Heritage Site with the rest of the Theban Necropolis.

There, Ancient Egypt's pharaohs were entombed deep underground into the heart of mountains. What is the significance of this? I will tell you more ...

Figure 41: Valley of the Kings – 640km (400 miles) south of the Great Pyramids of Giza, Egypt.

In southern Egypt's Valley of the Kings, in the 3,300-year-old tomb (KV17) of one of the founders of the New Kingdom's 19th Dynasty pharaoh Seti I (1314-1304 BCE), a descending underground tunnel of 195m (570 feet) long was discovered which took almost 40 years and multiple stages of strenuous efforts to excavate to the end of the tunnel. It is one of the best decorated tombs in the valley. This very long tunnel, known as corridor K, leads away deep into the mountainside from beneath the location where the sarcophagus stood in the burial chamber. See Figure 42.

Egyptian archaeologists believed the tunnel was meant to connect the 3,300-year-old pharaoh's tomb with a "secret burial site". After a few promising restarts to the project, eventually, at its last excavation, the tunnel came to its abrupt end. It turned out there was no "secret burial chamber" or any kind of burial chamber at the end of the long tunnel. Seti I's son Ramses II built many grand temples and statues of himself all across Egypt. It was speculated that Seti I's death stopped the construction of the tunnel and its secret tomb before completion. It was also speculated that Seti I's tunnel was meant to be a symbolic other-worldly journey to the hidden world of the underground god Sokar.

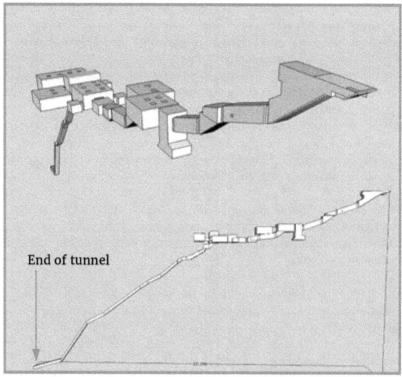

End of tunnel

Figure 42: King Seti I - 3D Schematic views of King Seti I's tomb in the Valley of the Kings, also known as KV17. The long descending tunnel could be seen in the bottom, showing the abrupt end of the tunnel.

What do I think? Alien Data Centers housing mega structures of super-computing crystals are the epicenters of eternal wisdom and universal knowledge throughout the cosmos. I think, it would be a fitting new journey of the afterlife for the great leaders of any ancient civilizations like the great pharaohs of ancient Egypt for their souls to be 'transmitted' to a nearby Alien Data Center and be reunited with its all-powerful symbols of alien consciousness and everlasting life 'housed' in its mega crystal structures.

Take a close look at Figure 43. The Theban Hills are dominated by the peak, the highest point is at 420m (1,400 feet), called the al-Qurn, known to ancient Egyptians as the "The Peak". Its ancient name is "Ta Dehent". When viewed from the entrance to the Valley of the Kings, "The Peak" looks almost pyramidal in structure. It is a natural formation shaped like a pyramid sitting majestically like a "crown" on the Valley of the Kings. Some Egyptologists believe that the appearance of "The Peak" is the important reason for choosing this site as the Royal Necropolis, the Valley for the Kings. In addition, this area was associated with the Egyptian goddess Hathor and the residence of the cobra goddess Meretseger (meaning "she who loves silence"). There is a plate-shaped rock formation projecting a few meters from the side of the hill giving the appearance of the spreading hood of the striking cobra.

The shape of pyramids is connected with the Sun god, Ra. According to ancient Egyptians, a pharaoh, upon death, will ascend to "heaven" to reunite with Ra. We know that crystals and prisms possess properties that can focus light, as we say light from the sun i.e. Ra, into a sharp focal point and can also spread light into various spectral components thus 'illuminating' the various realms of existence along the journey of the pharaoh's soul into Ra's heaven.

Is it a coincidence that pyramids are portrayed as rays of light shining from Ra above as a kind of blessing and as a sacred lighthouse to guide the souls of the pharaohs into "heaven"? I don't think it is a coincidence at all. I think it is a strong correlation to the pharaohs' fascination with the power of crystals.

I believe "The Peak" is actually meant to be the pyramidion or the 'single-termination point' (tip) of a giant crystal beam. I call it the "al-Qurn Crystal Obelisk", dedicated to Ra and as the instrument to enter Ra's "heavenly" kingdom. If we take the reference examples from Figure 6 and Figure 7, the total height of the "al-Qurn Crystal Obelisk" (assuming the height of al-Qurn to be 50m (166 feet 8 inch)) can be approximated to be about 500m (1,666 feet 8 inch) tall. "The Peak" is a natural rock formation with the giant long body of "al-Qurn Crystal Obelisk" buried vertically into the "al-Qurn" mountain. Millions of years of climatic changes could have accumulated tons of sand, debris, and rocks around the "al-Qurn Crystal Obelisk" and covered it up to the top of the crystal tip leaving only al-Qurn visible.

Figure 43: "The Peak" or al-Qurn - A natural pyramid-shaped structure at the top (outlined) of the Theban Hills at the entrance to the Valley of the Kings. "The Peak" is thought to be the pyramidion or the 'single-termination point' (tip) of a Giant Crystal Beam – the "al-Qurn Crystal Obelisk" buried into the mountain and hidden from view.

Alien Data Centers *are* "Super Crystal Caves" I wrote about in previous chapters. The "Cave of Crystals" was located in the Naica Mines, in Mexico, at a depth of about 300 meters (1,000 feet). I think what Seti I was trying to do was to 'aim' his tomb-tunnel to connect to a "Crystal Cave" presumably located there. To do so, he would have to dig even deeper, probably another 120-150m (400-500 feet) deeper to reach it. Alas, it was not easy to do so. Had Seti I succeeded, it is probable to imagine he would have achieved what no other pharaohs past, present or future could have accomplished. A Crystal-loving Obelisk-loving civilization finally connected with the universal Alien consciousness, with Ra, basking in the eternal existence with the secrets of the Universe, a worthy place amongst the Gods. Truly remarkable!

The makeup of organic lifeforms consists of a substantial amount of crystals. Human bodies are made of about 70% water which are crystals in nature. Could Alien Data Centers be found in organic lifeforms?

△ △ △

Human Crystals

Śarīras are Buddhist relics, in particular, they are crystal-like bead-shaped objects that are found among the cremated ashes and remains of the Buddha, Buddhist or Tibetan spiritual masters. Relics are an important aspect of forms of many religions. A relic usually consists of the physical remains of a venerated person preserved and worshipped for purposes of veneration as a tangible memorial.

Considered as relics of significant importance in many sects of Buddhism, Śarīras are believed to embody the spiritual knowledge, wisdom and manifestations of the once-living being. Śarīras are perceived as physical evidence of the masters' enlightenment and spiritual purity. Some believe the Śarīras are left with good intentions by the consciousness of a master to aid in the transference of knowledge and that the beauty of the Śarīras depends on how well the masters had cultivated their minds and souls.

Śarīras are generally displayed in a small glass vessel or stupas or could be enshrined in the master's statue. Śarīras come in a variety of colors and some are even translucent. They are also believed to mysteriously grow or increase in numbers if they have been stored under certain conditions inside their containers. It is well known that various religious faiths have adorned their religious artefacts with precious crystals, gems and Śarīras.

Śarīras are believed to emanate and incite 'blessings' and 'grace' within the "Mindstream[7]" and experiences of those connected with these relics. "Mindstream" is an evolution of the mind in terms of how individual minds continue from one's lifetime to the next, with Karma as the intervening mechanism disrupting the course of transformation from one life to the next.

---

[7] In Buddhist philosophy, "Mindstream" or "Stream of the Mind" is the moment-to-moment continuum of mind or awareness, ever flowing from one life to the next, likened to the flame of a candle being passed from one candle to another.

Figure 44: Śarīras – Human Crystals (left) remained after the cremation of enlightened spiritual Buddhist masters and of the Buddha himself. Śarīras of all shapes and sizes (right).

Crystals possess natural super properties which I have covered in previous chapters – quantum entanglement, quantum teleportation, timeless and unlimited energy source and much more. Could the Śarīra crystals have similar or other unknown metaphysical supernatural properties that scientists have not yet discovered? I have theorized that Alien Data Centers are made of crystals and are designed to process quantum information belonging to the existential plane. Could the Śarīra crystals be embedded with some kind of compact compressed ultra-high crystal memory forms of ancient wisdom and spiritual knowledge of the Universe, space and time?

Perhaps a scene, shown in Figure 45, from the Indiana Jones movie "Kingdom of the Crystal Skull" could help illustrate my theory. In the movie, interdimensional beings, a group of thirteen crystal skeletons which when combined, started 'firing' bolts of knowledge out of their Crystal Skulls into the eyes of a scientist who demanded to know the knowledge of everything. The method of knowledge transmission could most probably be via quantum entanglement (represented in cinematic style in the movie) as I have covered before. The knowledge transfer from the thirteen interdimensional beings began to overwhelm the scientist whose eyes ignited into flames eventually disintegrating the body. I think the scientist's internal crystalline structures in the brain and water-based crystalline body were not of the right kind of crystal formation nor strength, thus not able to contain all the amount of quantum-entangled information transferred across to it, thus leading to total disintegration of the host body. The thirteen skeletons then merged sequentially to form a single biological organic being which then entered a portal, in their dome-shaped flying saucer, opened up by some kind of quantum teleportation device.

Figure 45: Interdimensional beings – All made of crystals. Crystal Skulls filled with Alien wisdom and knowledge. (Indiana Jones-"Kingdom of the Crystal Skull")

The ***General Theory of Aliens (GTA)*** is Alien Data Centers are manufactured in planets that are ideal for making giant super crystal beams that are imbued with advanced high-tech properties. Ideal ingredients for super crystal manufacturing are a mixture of high heat (supplied by the planet's core), abundance of water (extremely rare and precious component in the universe, available on extremely small number of planets or planetary satellites) and the right kind of super crystal core materials. It is my belief that Alien Data Centers are amassed at places within or near to the "Ring of Fire", the factories of Giant Crystal Caves. It is also my belief that Alien Data Centers have bases that are still in operation in modern times. As there is no limit to the wonders of crystals, human crystals could be some kind of embedded Alien Data Centers, perhaps in a way, size does not matter, only knowledge does.

In the next chapter, I will provide the summary of my "General Theory of Aliens".

"AXIOM:HEART TREMORS sealing up water-filled caverns. Giant crystal beams instantly forming in orderly constructs minded by A'kira, a billion light years away, a billion lifetimes of wisdom."

9

General Theory of Aliens

✳

"Over the tides of millenniums, countless Minds thriving in countless Crystal Caves around the Universe. Forever vibrating with the Cosmic 'All-Seeing Consciousness'."

So many mysteries in the Universe yet to discover, so many star galaxies to explore, so many planets to walk on. So little time in one's lifetime to learn, so little to start on, yet so empowering if just to catch a little glimpse of the infinite. What better way to start than to have the hidden truths in our planet revealed at once to help us illuminate the way forward and outwards.

I set out on a personal journey to find the single version of truth to unite all theories about the Alien and UFO phenomena. Although I started with just an idea, I didn't know what I would find, or if I would find anything at all. I could come full 'circle' to my starting point. On my journey, I was touched by many interesting ideas, wonderful and so powerful that I feel inspired and motivated to share with my readers and fans. From that process, I strongly believe I have finally discovered the foundation of the unifying theory of Aliens which I set out to accomplish. I call it the "General Theory of Aliens" – GTA for short. GTA is made up of many revelations and insights that are supported by research, archeology, science, ancient history and a touch of educated imagination. In this chapter, I provide the framework of the GTA – the "General Theory of Aliens".

Safeguarding and preserving the existence of life, the minds and souls of every entity across the cosmos ought to be the highest motivation of any species, most definitely an Alien one. Aliens are adamant to ensure the fabric of wisdom and knowledge of life and existence to never cease, to continuously be transferred and never to be extinguished by the test of time and wills, to which end they would go to extreme efforts over millions of years to achieve that and to keep it going throughout all space and time.

Aliens have mastered the capabilities and knowledge of how to build out their Alien Data Centers, as large caves of giant Crystals, anywhere in the planet. Aliens learned to harness the super properties of crystals and knew how to grow their data centers in any pre-determined and pre-configured plan they desired. They infused every bit of their crystal data centers with various types of crystal to serve all multitudes of computing functions an advanced data center would need. Alien Data Centers are complete with super technological capabilities enabled by their manipulation of super crystalline properties, with highly-advanced patterns of crystal-to-crystal communication, of which their crystal infrastructures were genetically architected to operate with computing prowess beyond our wildest imaginations.

All over the ages and eons of civilizations, ancient natives were fascinated by the beauty and awe-inspiring forms of crystal beams and determinedly built giant pyramids to honor their "Alien Teachers" and longing to reunite with them in their afterlife. What they couldn't build they left clues so others can imagine what they would look like. Ancient people have experienced the super powers of crystals, and were compelled to create and build Giant Pyramids to represent Crystal Obelisks. National monuments and crystal structures that people from all walks of life would come to visit, experience and to marvel at. Potentially, setting off dreams and ideas in others too, like they have set me on.

Aliens had long mastered the science of harnessing the special properties of crystals. They have the advanced know-how to extend their properties to any object made out of crystals. Break a computer chip in a modern PC or smartphone today will destroy the function of that object. But make an object or device out of an Alien crystal beam will reproduce its master function and have the ability to 'program' new features, modify existing ones and even to self-repair, self-heal like crystals do. There have been many parallels with the crystal-based technologies of Aliens - our powerful and emotional stories of Superman and his "Fortress of Solitude" and we made beautiful skulls out of crystals. We have gone to great lengths to express our deep fascination with the powers of crystal.

The key technique critical to the construction of Alien Data Centers is based on manipulating the structures of crystals and exploiting all its super properties – we are only just starting to scratch the surface of what's possible. The key ingredient is Crystals! To be specific, Aliens connected a network of crystal beams that provided data center functions in myriad of capabilities to provide: unlimited energy source for crystal-powered lasers; a network of multi-qubit quantum computers; high-density storage; super-computing and information processing; super high-speed information sharing which means ultra-high-speed networking bandwidths; teleporting and transferring information across infinite distances instantaneously and effortlessly. A super important knowledge Aliens had was they utilized Time Crystals to unleash an unlimited source of energy to power all their data centers and crystal devices. Alien Data Centers are built upon a foundation of crystal-based infrastructure, of crystal-based intelligent computing equipment and devices.

Alien presence and the flight patterns of their "UFOs" have inspired ancient civilizations for thousands of years, possibly via personal encounters or projected visions. Alien UFOs possess superior aerial technologies that have prevented visual or digital detections and have cleverly utilized special properties of crystals to remain undetectable and invisible, and displayed cloaking capabilities. "Alien Teachers" had greatly motivated their ancient 'students' to such a great level that they were encouraged to make contact and to communicate with their revered teachers. Aliens had inspired ancient people to build beautiful and worthy monuments shaped like giant forms of crystals and function like solar calendars, and encoded them with universal mathematical formulas and constants into their architectures. To center their worship and philosophy, ancient people cleverly encoded the circular disk shapes of their teachers' flying spacecrafts to resemble the Sun and Moon and into their line of designs of advanced solstice calculations, and built mighty stone structures to express them. Aliens travelled in flying saucers of various forms – the most common shape is the dome-shape Saucer Type I and is the most regularly sighted object – that come with various functions as cosmic transporters of quantum crystal data and other quantum computing devices for their bases of Alien Data Centers. "Alien Teachers" transferred their advanced science and engineering, machinations and tools, agriculture, irrigation and more to worthy ancient civilizations. The latter built stone structures, be it laterally or vertically, with advanced engineering skills, not possible to replicate by today's tools, across Mesoamerican cities like Tiwanaku, Pumapunku, Chichen-Itza, Teotihuacan, and more.

Communicating with Ancient Aliens is still difficult but ancient civilizations never stopped trying, forever trying to make the first contact, with processes often taking thousands of years. Nevertheless, ancient civilizations found great strength and perseverance, exhibited supreme creativity in constructing monument-based forms of communications with their "Alien Teachers" and their UFOs. Ancient civilizations designed, built, and encoded messages of knowledge and science into the structural designs of their pyramids, stone circles, solar calendars and calculators and more. Ancient cultures designed their monuments to reflect their appreciation and worship of alien artefacts to resemble Obelisks, circular and dome shapes of their flying machines, and to explicitly and artistically display their knowledge of astronomical mathematical constants or Golden ratios. Many magnificent representations of Alien-worship structures are found across today's South American countries in Peru, Bolivia and Mexico, and of course in Egypt and England, and other places around the world, and even on Mars. And perhaps on other unknown planets.

The truth is Alien Data Centers are manufactured in planets which are ideal for making giant super high-tech crystal beams. Ideal ingredients for super crystal manufacturing are a mixture of high heat from magma, pockets of water and the right kind of crystal core materials. Alien Data Centers are amassed at places within or near the "Ring of Fire" – the factories of Giant Crystal Caves. Alien Data Centers have bases that are still in operation in modern times. As there is no limit to the wonders of crystals, human crystals could be host to some kind of alien data centers, perhaps in a way, size does not matter, only knowledge does.

The end-to-end architecture solution of the "General Theory of Aliens" can be expressed by Figure 46. The Alien Data Center, home to seven giant crystal obelisks, is powered by Time Crystals. Quantum UFOs enter the Crystal Cave with quantum-entangled information crystals and dock into the data center becoming part of the whole. To honor "Alien Teachers", ancient civilizations built many mathematically encoded monuments of stone circles, pyramids and obelisks.

And, finally ... I believe

We are All Crystals!

"Recurring throughout the Universe far and wide, the general solution guides every civilization every sentient entity onto the collective path of abundance Existence and Mind."

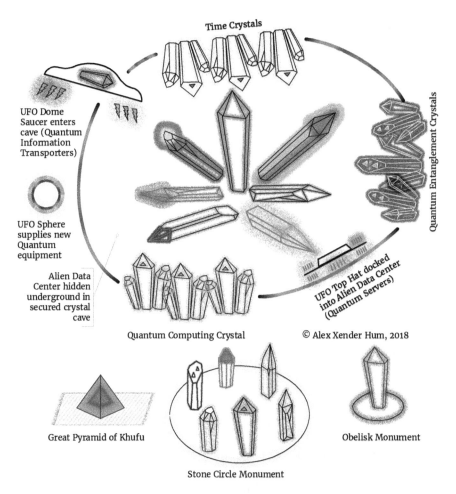

Time Crystals

Quantum Entanglement Crystals

UFO Dome Saucer enters cave (Quantum Information Transporters)

UFO Sphere supplies new Quantum equipment

Alien Data Center hidden underground in secured crystal cave

Quantum Computing Crystal

© Alex Xender Hum, 2018

UFO Top Hat docked into Alien Data Center (Quantum Servers)

Great Pyramid of Khufu

Stone Circle Monument

Obelisk Monument

Figure 46: Alien Data Center – In a giant crystal cave hidden underground, giant crystal beams operate with special quantum functions, crystallizing in pre-programed formations. UFO Saucer Type I entering cave (top) with a large quantum-entangled information crystal. UFO Sphere supplies new quantum equipment. UFO Top Hat docks its quantum server into the networked data center (center right). Infinite energy, powered by Time Crystals, flowing in cave enclosure drives all crystal functions. Seven giant crystal Obelisks (center) is "Alien Teacher". Ancient civilizations honor with amazing monuments (bottom). (Alex X. Hum)

Bibliography

Choi, S., Choi, J., Landig, R., Kucsko, G., Zhou, H., Isoya, J., . . . Lukin, M. D. (2017, March 8). Observation of discrete time-crystalline order in a disordered dipolar many-body. *nature.*

Conover, E. (2018, May 4). *'Time Crystals' Created in Two New Types of Materials.* Retrieved from Science News: https://www.sciencenews.org/article/time-crystals-created-two-new-types-materials

Dickerson, K. (2014, December 8). *Quantum Teleportation Reaches Farthest Distance Yet.* Retrieved from Live Science: https://www.livescience.com/49028-farthest-quantum-teleportation.html

Emspark, J. (2017, July 14). *Chinese Scientists Just Set the Record for the Farthest Quantum Teleportation.* Retrieved from LiveScience: https://www.livescience.com/59810-quantum-teleportation-record-shattered.html

Gramling, C. (2008, October 9). Danger and Wonder in Nat Geo's "Giant Crystal Cave". *Earth Magazine.* Retrieved from https://www.earthmagazine.org/article/danger-and-wonder-nat-geos-giant-crystal-cave

Kazansky, P., Cerkauskaite, A., Beresna, M., Drevinskas, R., Patel, A., Zhang, J., & Gecevicius, M. (2016, March 11). Eternal 5D Data Storage Via Ultrafast-Laser Writing In Glass. *The International Society for Optics and Photonics.*

Lee, K. M., Tondiglia, V. P., McConney, M. E., Natarajan, L. V., Bunning, T. J., & White, T. J. (2014, September 17). Color-Tunable Mirrors Based on Electrically Regulated Bandwidth Broadening in Polymer-Stabilized Cholesteric Liquid Crystals. *ACS Photonics, 1 (10),* pp. 1033-1041.

Lovgren, S. (2007, April 6). Giant Crystal Cave's Mystery Solved. *National Geographic News.* Retrieved from https://news.nationalgeographic.com/news/2007/04/070406-giant-crystals.html

Macdonald, F. (2017, Jan 28). Scientists Have Confirmed a Brand New Phase of Matter: Time Crystals. *Science Alert*. Retrieved from https://www.sciencealert.com/scientists-have-just-announced-a-brand-new-form-of-matter-time-crystals?utm_source=feedburner&utm_medium=feed&utm_campaign=Feed:+sciencealert-latestnews+(ScienceAlert-Latest)

Pal, S., Nishad, N., Mahesh, T., & Sreejith, G. (2018, May 1). Temporal Order in Periodically Driven Spins in Star-Shaped Clusters. *Physical Review Letters, 120, 180602.*

Rovny, J., Blum, R. L., & Barrett, S. E. (2018, May 1). Observation of Discrete-Time-Crystal Signatures in an Ordered Dipolar Many-Body System. *Physical Review Letters, 120, 180603.*

Sverdlik, Y. (2016, June 27). *Here's How Much Energy All US Data Centers Consume.* Retrieved from DataCenter Knowledge: https://www.datacenterknowledge.com/archives/2016/06/27/heres-how-much-energy-all-us-data-centers-consume

Sverdlik, Y. (2018, October 23). *Oracle Expanding New Cloud Platform to 13 Regions by 2019.* Retrieved from DataCenter Knowledge: https://www.datacenterknowledge.com/oracle/oracle-expanding-new-cloud-platform-13-regions-2019

Towers Point to Ancient Sun Cult. (2007, March 1). Retrieved from BBC News: http://news.bbc.co.uk/1/hi/sci/tech/6408231.stm

Vance, E. (2018, April 30). *These 'Spooky' Entangled Atoms Just Bought Quantum Computing One Step Closer.* Retrieved from Live Science: https://www.livescience.com/62433-most-entangled-qubits-quantum-computer.html

Wilczek, F. (2012, October 15). Quantum Time Crystal. *Physical Review Letters, 109, 160401.*

www.nationalgeographic.org. (n.d.). *Ring of Fire.* Retrieved from National Geographic: https://www.nationalgeographic.org/encyclopedia/ring-fire/

Yao, N., Potter, A., Potirniche, I.-D., & Vishwanath, A. (2017, January 18). Discrete Time Crystals: Rigidity, Criticality, and Realizations. *Physical Review Letters, 118 030401.*

Zhang, J., Hess, P. W., Kyprianidis, A., Becker, P., Lee, A., Smith, J., . . . Monroe, C. (2017, March 8). Observation of a Discrete Time Crystal. *nature.*

Index

www.ingramcontent.com/pod-product-compliance
Lightning Source LLC
LaVergne TN
LVHW041214050326
832903LV00021B/611